PRAISE FOR
MiDLIFE BiTES

"Thank you, Jen Mann, for writing *the* manual on middle-age in the most authentic, relatable way ever. I inhaled this book in one sitting. Jen's writing is fresh, funny, fearless, and fantastic. *Midlife Bites* is more than a book—it's a movement, and a must-read for anyone over forty. This should become the gift all girlfriends give one another. Thanks, Jen, for making me feel less alone, entertaining me, and telling it like it is. Preach!"
—ZIBBY OWENS, host of the award-winning podcast *Moms Don't Have Time to Read Books*

"One part instruction manual (or maybe destruction manual?), one part group therapy, and all kinds of hilarious, *Midlife Bites* made the prospect of hitting my midforties seem a lot more manageable and a lot less mystifying. Jen Mann is leading the midlife revolution and I am *so* here for it!"
—SARAH KNIGHT, *New York Times* bestselling author of *The Life-Changing Magic of Not Giving a F*ck*

"If you've ever felt like you're screaming into the void alone, you're not. Jen Mann is there. Admittedly and masterfully out of her comfort zone, Jen comes at her midlife self with a wallop of self-introspection and vulnerability, thereby giving all of us permission to say the paralyzing quiet parts out LOUD. Every woman who reads this book will say thank you, Jen Mann, in between snorts and sniffles."

—FAITH SALIE, author of *Approval Junkie* and panelist on NPR's *Wait Wait . . . Don't Tell Me!*

BALLANTINE BOOKS BY JEN MANN

People I Want to Punch in the Throat

*Spending the Holidays with
People I Want to Punch in the Throat*

Midlife Bites

MiDLiFE BiTES

MiDLiFE BiTES

*Anyone Else Falling Apart
or Is It Just Me?*

JEN MANN

BALLANTINE BOOKS   NEW YORK

Published in the United States by Ballantine Books,
an imprint of Random House, a division of
Penguin Random House LLC, New York.

BALLANTINE and the HOUSE colophon are registered trademarks
of Penguin Random House LLC.

LIBRARY OF CONGRESS CATALOGING-IN-PUBLICATION DATA
Names: Mann, Jen, author.
Title: Midlife bites : anyone else falling apart or is it just me? / Jen Mann.
Description: New York : Ballantine Books, [2022]
Identifiers: LCCN 2020057418 (print) | LCCN 2020057419 (ebook) | ISBN
9780593158517 (trade paperback) | ISBN 9780593158524 (ebook)
Subjects: LCSH: Middle-aged women. | Midlife crisis—Humor.
Classification: LCC HQ1059.4 .M36 2022 (print) | LCC HQ1059.4 (ebook) | DDC
305.244/2—dc23
LC record available at https://lccn.loc.gov/2020057418
LC ebook record available at https://lccn.loc.gov/2020057419

Printed in the United States of America on acid-free paper

randomhousebooks.com

2 4 6 8 9 7 5 3 1

Book design by Diane Hobbing

This book is dedicated to every exhausted, mildly irritated middle-aged woman who doesn't have time to read this book, but really should.

CONTENTS

AUTHOR'S NOTE

All of the names, circumstances, and midlife crises in this book have been changed to protect the good, the bad, and the ugly. These are my stories and this is how I remember them. You might remember them differently.

INTRODUCTION

Several years ago, when I started my blog, "People I Want to Punch in the Throat," it was a place where I could blow off steam, tell funny stories about myself, the Hubs, and my kids, Gomer and Adolpha (I swear their real names are worse), write about life in general, and say all the things everyone thinks but never mentions out loud. A few months into blogging, I wrote a post about the Elf on the Shelf that went viral to more than a million people in a little over twenty-four hours, launching my writing career. Over the years I've used my blog as a place to process my emotions and opinions, and the substantial online platform I've built acts as a megaphone to share those feelings. So with my forty-seventh birthday looming, and some tough stuff going on in my life, I began to wonder,

"Am I having a midlife crisis? And what does that even look like for women?"

I turned to my online community and wrote the blog post "Anyone Else Falling Apart or Just Me?" describing how I felt and wondering out loud (on the Internet) if others were feeling the same way. Most of what I write is funny or snarky. I'm a chronic complainer. No one would ever call me perky, but this was a definite departure from my normal fare. Feeling a bit lost and overwhelmed, I hadn't blogged for several months and my readership was down, so I didn't really expect many people to care about the post. This time I wasn't writing for page views, I was writing to help me understand my feelings and what I was going through.

I'd written the post in the predawn hours, well before my alarm was scheduled to go off. I always do my best and most honest writing in the middle of the night, when there are few distractions and few inhibitions. No matter what I'm writing about, I always try to be honest and truthful. But sometimes I leave out the most painful stuff—not everything is for public consumption. I'd written the post on my laptop in bed, buried under the covers, with tears and snot streaming down my face, a hot mess, surrounded by wadded-up used tissues. The Hubs was out of town and my kids were still asleep. I was alone.

When I finished writing I held my breath for a second before I hit Publish. This was the first (and only) time when I was so raw and vulnerable about something other than my outrage at despicable behavior or general bullshit. I didn't even try to sugarcoat it or crack a badly timed joke. I just laid myself bare, while at the same time wondering if this might be the end of my career. I took a deep breath and hit the button.

ANYONE ELSE FALLING APART OR JUST ME?

People I Want to Punch in the Throat blog post, July 8, 2019

So I'm pretty sure I'm going through a midlife crisis. I feel like I'm falling apart. I feel like the more I try to keep from falling apart, the faster I fall apart. I feel like I'm drowning and I can't breathe. And, on top of all that, I also feel numb. I'm not positive that's a midlife crisis, because when I Google midlife crisis or signs of a midlife crisis, so much of the information points to how men feel or how men can cope. There's not a lot of information out there for women.

I thought, Maybe it doesn't happen to us? No, I think it's more like we don't talk about this stuff.

I was reminded of a story about my overwhelmed great-grandmother asking her doctor for some help and he told her, "Nice women don't discuss such things."

Nice women don't discuss such things.

I guess it's a good thing I'm not a nice woman? Because I'm ready to discuss this uncomfortable topic.

I'm miserable. I've been feeling this way for about a year now and I was afraid to say anything even to my closest friends and family. It's a really shitty thing to say out loud, because I know it hurts the people close to me, plus it just sounds like typical suburban angst. If I was a refugee somewhere, I wouldn't get the luxury to say, "I'm just not happy." I'm not running for my life, I'm not watching people around me get murdered, I don't have any real strife in my life, so what the fuck? Buck up! Right?

I don't know, though. Don't I deserve to be happy? Don't I owe it to myself? Isn't that what I'm always preaching? Or am

I supposed to keep this all to myself and just muddle through and not make waves?

Yes, I'm really unhappy and dissatisfied with my life. I've passed forty-five and I feel like it's all downhill now. I find myself asking on a daily basis, "Is this it? Is this all there is?"

Which, again, is a really shitty thing to ask, because I know my life is not horrible. And then that makes me feel even worse. Like I'm not grateful for all that I have or all that I've accomplished.

I am grateful, I just . . . want more. I expected more. It's just that by my mid-forties I expected to be further along in my career. I expected more security. I expected a different relationship. And I'm not a perfectionist or a high-achiever by any stretch of the imagination, but I guess I set some lofty goals for myself and when I didn't reach them it sort of sent me into a spiral. I feel like I'm constantly scrabbling to hang on to what I have and I can barely advance. It feels like every time I get it figured out, someone moves the finish line on me. I feel like I wasted my twenties doing stupid shit when I should have been working harder, smarter, faster, whatever. Maybe if I'd done that, I'd be in a better position now? I don't know. I keep reliving past decisions and fretting over the choices I made. And that's not helping. I used to be able to take those regrets and that fear and turn it into something productive, but now I just let it drag me down.

My husband founded a start-up a few years ago and he's been working really hard at that, but it's not taking off as fast as either of us would like. It's very demanding on his time and he's not able to help me as much as he used to. He's also not able to work at his "real" job as much, so the pressure has been on me to produce even more and support the family.

I've been dealing with health problems for the last year and a half and it's been financially and emotionally and physically taxing. After twenty-plus years together, I feel like the passion is gone from my marriage. Don't get me wrong, the Hubs and I were never tearing each other's clothes off in public, but lately, my marriage feels like a business arrangement. We're great partners, but we don't talk about anything other than our work. That's not how it used to be. Maybe we've run out of conversation? My kids are getting older and I worry if I've done a good job raising them. I never had doubts about my parenting before and they're not doing anything to make me question their upbringing and yet, I can't shake that somehow I've fucked them up and they won't be contributing members of society. When my kids were small, I felt like I lost my identity because I was suddenly "Mom" and no longer "Jen." I wasn't young or interesting anymore. Now that my kids are older, I'm losing my "Mom" identity. What will I be in a few short years when they go off to college? Do I go back to being "Jen"? An even older and less interesting person?

I don't sleep well anymore, I cry and I'm irritable. I haven't felt funny in months. The last time I felt this way was years ago. And that's why I started this blog. I was feeling a ton of pressure and incredibly overwhelmed by my life and I started writing here. I found my sanity, I found my people, and I found a career for myself.

Writing is my way to deal with stress and pain in my life, but this time I've kept it all bottled up inside of me. I haven't hardly blogged in a year and when I do, it's always about frivolous bullshit rather than what I'm really feeling. I've always said I didn't care what people thought about me and what I write, but this year I cared. I've always said I'm an open book and I tell it like it is, but this year, I kept a lot to myself. Because for the first time I was ashamed of how I felt. I was worried about hurting the people I care about most with my honesty. I was worried about what strangers will think of me. I was worried about looking like a failure, or worse, a complainer.

Well, I'm done doing that. I'm sitting here, spitting it all out on the page through tears. I am releasing everything here and letting it all go because I think I will explode if I keep this inside any longer.

Last week I told my friends how I was feeling. It was with trepidation that I asked if anyone else was feeling like they were losing their shit. I was terrified they'd tell me I was crazy. That I have a great life and I need to suck it up and stop feeling sorry for myself, or whatever. Instead, they opened up and shared their own feelings and I realized I was not alone.

I can't tell you the relief this brought me.

I look around and I see men my age buying sports cars, getting hair plugs, and dating twenty-something women. What do women do when they're going through this? From what I can tell, we suffer in silence.

We are the ones who plaster on fake smiles, or at least neutral faces, and go about the business of getting shit done, even though we're screaming inside. We're the ones who take care of our parents, our children, and our husbands. We're the ones who make sure everyone has what they need. We're the ones who care for everyone else, except ourselves. We're the ones who don't talk about our feelings of loneliness, fear, inadequacy, bankruptcy, or whatever, because we're afraid we'll sound selfish or we're afraid of being judged. And, frankly, we don't have time to wallow.

I finally broke down and told my husband how I was feeling. It wasn't some big revelation. He's not stupid. He'd noticed the change in me. He'd felt me pull away from him, from our life. I was disengaged and going through the motions and he could tell, he just didn't know what to do to help me. The advice he gave me was, "You need to write about this." His advice was solid.

Even now, as I come to the end of this post, I'm feeling better. It feels good to be open and honest and to be truthful about my feelings of sadness. I'm not cured by any stretch of the imagination, but I do feel better. Putting my thoughts and feelings onto paper has always been my form of therapy. It has always been how I process hard things. I'd gotten away from that this year and I want to get back to it. I won't worry about how many page views I get or the SEO I need to bring traffic to this post, because that shit doesn't matter. What matters is that the people who need to see this and hear this find this post.

If you recognize yourself in what I've written here, then just know you are not alone. You don't have to be miserable in silence. You are not broken or selfish. You are normal. I understand you and I see you. I know it hurts and I know that you worry about hurting those around you, but you have to make yourself the priority right now. It's time for us to put on our oxygen masks first. You're not helping anyone by keeping it all inside. And you're not fooling anyone. We have to speak up and we have to let the people in our lives know how they can help us.

I'd like to wrap this up in a bow and give you all a happy ending and some great advice, but I'm not there yet. Right now I don't know what to do to help me. I know self-care is key. Figuring out what will recharge me and help me cope. Like I said, just writing this was an immense relief and that tells me that I need to keep doing that. Just getting back to writing whatever is on my mind is a comfort.

I also need to find my funny again. I used to be able to find the humor in everything hard, but right now I'm not finding any humor. I rack my brain every day trying to come up with something funny to write about. I'm shocked when I actually laugh out loud and it's such an overwhelming sense of relief and a high, but it's fleeting. It's just tough to be funny or find funny right now, but I'm determined to do it again. I've always said, "You're going to laugh or cry, so you might as well laugh." Well, I've cried enough and I'm ready to laugh again.

—Jen Mann

I waited nervously for my readers' reactions. I knew this post was different. It wasn't just a typical opinion piece where I could defend my take or write about something tough with scathing commentary. This one was personal to me and emotional. Based on my current state of mind, I didn't know if I could handle any backlash. But, honestly, what could someone say to me that I hadn't already said to myself? I braced myself for the first of many comments like *"Seriously? These are the most first-world problems I've ever heard, Jen!"* or *"Grow up, Jen!"* or *"Have you tried essential oils?"*

I pulled up Google Analytics to see how many people were reading the post. My ego was torn: Yes, negative comments would hurt me, but it would absolutely destroy me if no one read what I put out there. What can I say? I'm a goddamn enigma.

The numbers were high. Really high. The heat map was lighting up and I could see that the post was being read all over the world.

And then the comments started rolling in and I was relieved to see not one mention of essential oils:

"You are definitely not alone. Every day, as soon as I wake up, I immediately think about when I can go back to bed. I don't want to participate any more. I feel like my friendships are slipping away. I'm not sad, that's not the right word to use. It's more of feeling like useless, or worn out. Like I've served my purpose and been cast aside."   —Kristen

"You are not alone. Last year after dealing with something similar I just walked out of my life with the purpose of finding me again, finding happy."   —KayLynn

"Thank you so so much for this! I needed this. I needed to hear that I'm not alone."   —Jenni

"This sounds an awful lot like me for the last few years."   —Angela

"I completely get what you are saying. I'm 48. For a long time I was everyone's caregiver, parents, kids, husband. In a very short period of time, 3 older relatives I took care of were gone and my teenager kids became assholes. I didn't, and still don't know what to do with myself or how to take care of myself. Like you, my life is good, but I totally feel like I messed up all my chances and ended up in a place that is less than my potential." —thinkpos

"As I read this I thought somehow you got into my mind, my life, my marriage, and my home and wrote about what you saw." —Tammy

"Thank you for sharing. Thank you for your honesty. Thank you for the words I have been unable to find." —Anonymous

"I am so grateful I decided to click on this and give it a read . . . I feel like there is a tribe out there. I'm 47 and between health issues that are serious but not deadly and a marriage that is more than likely ending after 23 years . . . I'm wrecked . . . Thank you for writing down what obviously many are feeling as well." —Anonymous

"Jen, I feel like you know exactly what I am going through . . . Thank you for writing this important piece and beginning the conversation . . . " —Deborah

"I feel like you have been living inside of my head for the past 4 years . . . Sharing in hopes someone else is feeling it too." —Theresa

The huge and immediate response was amazing. I felt an instant call to action. In the past, I'd found success creating a community of like-minded parents, and I knew then it was time to create another community, this time one for women "of a certain age," essentially forty to sixty, who were experiencing the same thing I was. I understood how lonely and lost I felt, and now I realized there were no doubt many other women out there who were feeling the same way. I realized that I had to create a new space where middle-aged women could share openly and honestly with one another. We all have a right to be happy. To be fulfilled. To feel whole. To have our ailments and physical (and mental) concerns diagnosed and treated properly. We should not feel embarrassed or weird talking about our feelings or the changes in our bodies with our families, with our doctors, or with one another. We should not treat this stage of our lives like a dirty little secret that "nice women" don't talk about. It's time to start the conversation about the physical and emotional struggles of middle-aged women, and I volunteer myself as tribute! I knew it was important, because I immediately felt better when my readers reached out to me and shared their stories. Thank you so much to everyone who supported me. It comforted me then, and it comforts me now, to have you share your experience and knowledge with me. You are the inspiration behind my writing this book.

Midlife Bites offers a glimpse into the journey I've been on for the past year and a half. I'm going to be as honest and open with you as I can here, because I need to be open and honest with myself. It's not going to be easy. I'm going to have to *feel* some shit. I'm going to have to break down some of my walls and let you in. I'm going to have to test my boundaries and try new things. All of this will hurt a little. Actually, if I do it right, it's going to hurt a lot. But it has to be done because we all know growth is painful, and I need to do some growing.

Having walked this path with you and ahead of you, I hope that in the end, this book will be of use to you, because let's face it, I'm full of great fucking advice! I'll drop some pearls of wisdom, some gems, tell you what worked for me and also what sucked balls for me but, who knows, might work for you. I'll let you see that you're not the first woman to have a midlife crisis, nor will you be the last. This is something that every generation has dealt with, but Generation X, and hopefully those that follow, will do it differently. Our mothers and grandmothers went through midlife without an online community to rely on, but my generation understands the value of a well-connected virtual gang of females hell-bent on supporting one another. We know that when we help one another, hard things become easier. We raised our children in the digital age, and with the help of online parenting groups, we formed bonds with strangers who ended up being some of our closest friends, those we could rely on the most. We found people who understood our struggles, who guided us through the rough patches, and then we turned around and reached back for the women behind us so we could help them in turn. We're going to do that again. Only this time instead of sharing potty training tips or ways to sneak veggies into our kids' meals, we're going to give solid advice about hot flashes, boob sweat, chin hairs, mood swings, sex swings, and hormone therapy.

Welcome to my world!

Love, Jen

MiDLiFE BiTES

How the Hell Did I Get Here?

I don't know about you, but for me, midlife came out of nowhere and kicked me square in my lady garden.

To tell the truth, I thought I'd dodged that whole midlife slump I'd caught older women whispering about when they didn't think I was listening. I was a late bloomer and really didn't come into my own until my thirties, so by the time I landed on forty, I was actually feeling great. A few years before, I'd started a blog called "People I Want to Punch in the Throat," which ultimately helped me develop my career as a writer, something I'd dreamed about since I was five years old. I was married to a man who adored me. My kids were pretty cool, and, most important, everyone was finally potty-trained. And most important of all, everyone was healthy. I lived in a nice home in a safe community where I tooled around in a sweet-ass minivan I'd bought myself with my own money. From the outside it looked like I had a great fucking life.

But then one morning I woke up with a groan (because it seemed like once I hit forty-five I never woke up again without a groan) and took a long, painfully honest look in the mirror. Something I hadn't done in quite some time. Every wrinkle, every gray hair, every soft and sagging body part came into sharp focus. I grimaced and finally noticed my bathroom counter was littered with miracle creams and serums, reading glasses, vitamins, and assorted prescription drugs for recently diagnosed ailments I thought only grandmothers suffered from.

I tried to focus on the positive: I've never been a stunner, so fading looks shouldn't bother me too much, I reasoned. I've always been praised for my . . . my what? Oh, yeah, my quick wit. Only that was fading too. Shit. When did my brain turn into a bowl of lukewarm oatmeal? (I would later try to blame my foggy brain on the prescription cocktail I take for my old lady disease, but my doctor assured me my brain wasn't in danger because the side effects would only destroy my liver. So, yay?)

I popped a handful of drugs plus my daily Aleve into my mouth and muttered, "When the hell did this happen?"

I looked at my phone, as if Google might have an answer for me. Instead, I saw my overstuffed calendar mocking me with a message in all caps announcing my forty-seventh birthday just a few days away.

Forty-seven already? It hit me that I was in the middle of my life (probably even past the middle if I wanted to get *real* depressing) and when I took stock of all the things I'd accomplished and accumulated over those forty-seven years, I felt incredibly underwhelmed. Half my life was over in a blink, and what did I have to show for it? *Is this all there is?*

For months, maybe even years, I'd been ignoring the slow, simmering buildup of my emotions, but that day it felt different. That day I couldn't ignore them and I couldn't stop them from boiling over. Before I could say "Shut it down!" I felt the floodgates open. All the thoughts and feelings I'd turned a blind eye to and had been pushing down deep daily, tumbled out all at once.

My brain might be foggy, but it can still be a real asshole. That day my brain was a total asshole.

It's all downhill from here, Jen.

What the fuck are you doing with your life?

What have you accomplished?

How will you retire? Have you seen your bank account? I know you made money. Where the hell did it go?

Have you seen what your neighbor Elizabeth has done? She runs her own company plus she founded a charity this year. Oh, and let's not forget, she still finds time for daily workouts to keep her body rocking, plus weekly date nights, and mind-blowing sex with her smoking-hot husband. When was the last time you had anything mind-blowing that wasn't a dessert? Do you even re-member how to do sex, Jen?

Furthermore, she's a supermom who still reads to her kids every night before bed. Yeah, they're fourteen and sixteen, but they want to spend time with her. When was the last time your kids wanted anything from you except money, Jen?

Is this it? Is this all you're going to do? Wasn't there supposed to be more? You had bigger plans than a minivan, a couple sassy kids, and a grumpy husband, didn't you?

Why did you waste so much time? Was watching the entire series of Friends *twice really worth it?*

Should you cut your bangs? Bangs always make you feel better. Well, really, the idea *of bangs makes you feel better. Because bangs always look awful on you. Don't cut your bangs—or do. Maybe this time will be different . . . what do you have to lose?*

Why are you so unhappy?

Why are you so mad? Seriously. This amount of anger isn't normal.

When did you start feeling this way?

Why is this happening?

You're the only one who feels like this, Jen. You're all alone. You're obviously broken.

I was falling apart. Losing my mind. Going crazy. Whatever you want to call it. I was spiraling out of control and couldn't stop. I was paralyzed by the fear of moving forward and the disappointment of what had already passed me by. I was consumed with the idea that I'd already failed and there was nothing I could do to make it better. What was the point? The "good" years were behind me and now I was "too old" to do anything amazing. Nope. All I could look forward to was old age and death.

And then, in case I wasn't feeling bad enough, along came the shame for even feeling this way.

Are you kidding me right now with this shit? What is going on with you, Jen?

Did I miss something?

Are you living in a tent?

Are you running for your life?

Are you in an abusive relationship?

Are you chronically ill?

Are you dying?

Is your child dying?

No! Of course not. You're wallowing! *There are so many people out there who have it worse than you. Who do you think you are? What makes you think you're so special? What makes you think you deserve more? There are people who would kill for your life, you tiny, self-absorbed, insufferable cow. You need to buck the fuck up, Buttercup, put on that happy face and just be grateful for what you have!*

Let's get real, it's not like I ever thought I'd cure cancer or broker world peace, but I did think that by this point in my life I'd have *done* more. I thought I'd *have* more. More love. More passion. More life experience. More money in the bank. More success. More friends. More self-worth. More happiness. More *everything*.

And weren't you supposed to have your shit together by forty-seven? Forty-seven is a serious age for serious women. Women who are forty-seven have robust retirement accounts, keep their cars properly maintained, and floss daily. Women who are forty-seven order side salads instead of fries and have a contact in their phone for everything from gutter cleaning to math tutors to bikini waxing to marriage counselors. Women who are forty-seven throw enormous parties to celebrate twenty-five years of wedded bliss and say things like they can't wait for another twenty-five years—and mean it!

I couldn't even match my bra and underpants on a daily basis, how was I expected to have my entire life sorted?

And while some of it was my fault because I'd wasted the first thirty years of my life on bad perms, dating fuckwits, working at dead-end jobs, and watching the entire series of *Friends* not twice, but *three* times, actually, I had to hand over some of the responsibility for my general malaise and lack of accomplishments to the universe. I'd tried doing things the right way, but no matter what I did, I found I could never get ahead, and I was drowning. Due to the shitty economy we'd survived and my equally shitty spending habits, we were nowhere near as financially sound as other forty-seven-year-olds. My marriage was relatively solid, but at that point the Hubs and I were more like business partners or roommates than lovers. The spark was dimming, if not completely extinguished. I felt like a failure in every aspect of my life. My teenage kids would be leaving home soon and I'd no longer have that buffer between me and him. How would we fill the silence in our house? What would we talk (and fight) about once the kids went to college? Oh, God, even worse, what if the kids never left home? I worried that I hadn't prepared them to fly the nest. That I hadn't raised contributing members of society. What if they took up permanent residence in my basement and refused to budge from the couch except for the occasional bathroom break or to get more snacks?

Where did all of this anxiety and self-doubt come from? I wondered. If anything, I'd been a cocky bitch for the previous ten years, and suddenly I couldn't sleep at night because on top of financial woes, relationship problems, and impostor syndrome, I was worried about dumb shit too, like whether Delia from fifth grade was still mad at me for stealing her favorite pencil. And don't even get me started on my lack of ambition. I mean, I barely wanted to get out of bed and take a shower, let alone go anywhere. If it required putting on pants or a bra, I wasn't going. It wasn't worth the effort to make myself presentable and to engage in mindless small talk with people I didn't even like very much.

I didn't feel like going anywhere, unless someone was inviting me to a revolution where I could burn shit to the ground. I'd put on pants for that! The one emotion I could still feel was rage, and all I could think about was annihilation. Not the annihilation of people, exactly. Just all the shit that goes with being an adult woman in this world. Sometimes it's too much for us to bear so we shut down to protect ourselves. But we sometimes go too far and lose all sensation. I think Cheryl burned down her own she-shed just so she could *feel* something.

I was angry, disappointed, sad, and confused. *Is this a midlife crisis?* I wondered.

Of course, I'd heard of midlife crises, but I assumed those were reserved for men. We've all known middle-aged guys who bought sports cars, gym memberships, and hair plugs and left their wives for a twentysomething waitress.

But what about the ladies? What would a female midlife crisis look like? I never knew a woman who ran off with her hot young man-bunned yoga instructor and started a new life. I'm not even sure that's what we want. When I think of running away, it's always to a secluded cabin in the woods with strong wifi and pizza delivery. Is that a midlife crisis? Do women even have midlife crises? Do they in fact exist for women? Was that what I was feeling? Oh shit, maybe it was! Well, that's just great. One more thing to add to my already out of control to-do list. I didn't have time for this. Maybe I could squeeze it in between getting Gomer to baseball practice, helping Adolpha with her pre-engineering homework, fixing dinner, blowing my husband's . . . er . . . mind, and writing the next chapter of my book! I figured I could at least fit in a few solitary moments when I could have a good cry in the garage after taking the dog to the vet. He'd never tell anyone about my breakdown in the minivan.

But every day that I ignored my feelings, I felt worse. My emotions were fluctuating by the hour. If I wasn't screaming at my family, I was sobbing or staring hopelessly at the wall. I've always been a fairly pissed off, lazy kind of person, but even I knew that what I was feeling wasn't normal.

Finally, I went looking for answers, or at least someone to commiserate with. I didn't come up with much. There weren't many books at the library I could read or podcasts I could listen to for helpful information. If other women were feeling like me, they were doing a great job hiding it, medicating it, and/or denying it.

At my yearly checkup, I asked my gynecologist what was happening to me. He's an older man who has seen me through two pregnancies and numerous IUDs. At every visit for the past fifteen years he's shamelessly asked me about my weekend plans while elbow-deep in my love canal, but when I mentioned that my emotions were out of control, he was clearly uncomfortable and had no real advice for me. This is a man who can talk to me at length about alarming lumps in my breasts or embarrassing hemorrhoids with care and compassion and sound advice, but this conversation was obviously too much for him. He grimaced and patted me on the arm and said, "Sounds a lot like you're entering menopause."

"Menopause?" I asked, wiping away tears. "Aren't I too young?"

He shrugged. "Well, you're forty-seven now. You're old

enough." He avoided eye contact and busied himself with tidying up the room. This was a first. It was always the nurse's job to clean everything up. "Don't worry. It's normal. It will pass."

"When?" I asked, my eyes wide and brimming with fresh tears.

He looked at the floor. "Could be five to . . . fifteen . . ."

I closed my eyes and hoped he was going to say *days*.

". . . years."

Years? Fuuuuuu. . . .

He patted my arm again. "Like I said, it's very normal. All women go through it."

"What can be done?" I asked.

He frowned. "There are options. None are great. But you should do some research on your own, and let's talk at next year's appointment and see if you're still feeling this way." And then he was gone.

Next year? What? Fuck you, man! Don't pat me! Fix me! Help me navigate this nightmare.

I realized at that moment that help wasn't coming. I was going to have to do this myself. And the hell I was going to wait a decade for it "to pass"! If men experienced perimenopause or menopause they'd have drive-thru clinics to deal with this shit. There'd be an entire section of the bookstore dedicated to the "mysteries of manopause." Female doctors wouldn't give them a condescending pat and say, "This too shall pass, honey."

That's the moment I decided I needed to start talking about what I was experiencing. With my friends, with my husband, with my community, with anyone who would listen. Men would never quietly go out to pasture and neither would I.

JEN'S GEMS

Hell yes, there is such a thing as a female midlife crisis. And hell yes, you're probably in the throes of one right now. And no, you're not alone. And hell yes, you should definitely try crying alone in the garage. It's surprisingly therapeutic!

Tap Tap Tap. Anybody Out There?

Finding Your People

> Honestly, I come here because no one in my real
> life will tell me like it is.
>
> —Nicole

It might take a kick in the ass to get me going, but once I decide to speak up about something, there's no shutting me up. Pair that with the fact that creating online communities is my thing, and I was off and running. Now, I know a lot of people feel anxious or overwhelmed on the Internet, and sometimes it can be a cesspool, but thankfully I'm able to weed through the shit and find the good stuff. And if I can't find what I want, I create it myself. I prefer to form groups that attract the people I'm looking for, rather than try and fit myself in to a group that may not be exactly what I'm looking for. I'm not for everybody and my groups aren't for everybody. If you don't like my group, that's fine. I encourage you to start your own.

Before I wrote my midlife crisis blog post, I was managing several different online communities. Some were for parents.

Some were for writers. Some were for book lovers. Some were for people who wanted to talk about politics. Some were for people who simply needed to laugh. There was something for everyone. Except I didn't have a space dedicated entirely to middle-aged women where they could talk privately about everything they were enduring as they aged. The response to my blog post was so immense that I knew women would quickly join a safe space where they would feel comfortable talking about both their physical and their emotional symptoms and concerns. A place where they could commiserate with one another but also find hope from the wisdom and experience of the women they were surrounded by.

I typically shoot from the hip, so I didn't have a real plan of attack when I created a private group on Facebook called Midlife Bites. I came up with the name because I wanted to attract women who were like me. No matter what I'm naming, I try to pick something that will let you know right away if you're my people or not. I thought the tweak on the title of the classic 1994 movie *Reality Bites* would speak to my fellow Generation X ladies and let them know that this was a place for them. I also try to make my names witty and a bit sharp. Midlife Bites fit the bill perfectly, because let's face it, midlife does indeed bite.

When I first created the group I added a few friends (against their will) and hoped they'd get hooked before they could bail. The secret to an excellent group is not really finding members. If you have a kick-ass group, the members will find you. But you have to make that group amazeballs by providing great content to keep them engaged and entertained.

Everyone knows great content when they see it, but it's super-difficult to just invent it. Contrary to popular belief, I don't just pull awesome shit out of my ass each day. I have to actually brainstorm it. So I was racking my brain trying to figure out what I could do to get the Midlife Bites conversation started. I wanted the women in the group to feel they could be honest and open, but I knew it might be awkward at the beginning because it can be scary to share in front of a group of strangers. I needed to find just the right topic to stimulate the conversation and get everyone to open up.

I put up a few generic icebreakers to try and get the members chatting while I worked on crafting the most absolutely perfect content to kick off the discussion. While I was mind-mapping potentially genius ideas, the discussion in the group turned to the heat wave many of us found ourselves trapped in. For a lot of us, that July was our first summer enduring hot flashes, and none of us were coping well.

The conversation was flowing and I was excited to keep it going. I wanted to present more to the group than my opinion that "Hot flashes in July fucking blow," so I went off to find actual sciencey advice that could help us all manage our suffering.

Suddenly, my notifications blew up on my phone. *Ding! Ding! Ding!* I could see they all were coming from Midlife Bites, so I clicked over to see what was happening. Comments and reactions were going crazy, plus there was a wait list of dozens of women queued up and waiting to join.

"What is going on?" I mumbled as I searched the group.

And then I saw the cause of all the commotion.

A woman I did not know (I still don't know who invited her to Midlife Bites or how she found it, but either way, I'm so grateful she did) had posted a photo, and the comments were pouring in. I took a closer look. The photo was of a glass dildo with little nubbies up and down the . . . uh . . . shaft. The woman who posted it wrote: "This helps me . . . not pleasure but hot nights . . . I went to a party and the hostess offered advice. Since the vaginal canal controls our body temperature I sometimes have to pull this from the back of the freezer. I pop it in and the cooldown starts. When I travel I fill condoms up with ice."

My brain just about exploded. *What the fuck? A frozen dildo for hot flashes?* I couldn't decide if it was brilliant or blasphemy.

This woman did not claim to be a medical professional of any kind and I had no clue if what she said was even remotely scientifically true, but I figured a frozen dildo in the honey pot wasn't much different from an ice cube, right? I quit clutching my pearls, took a deep breath, and chucked the very helpful (but boring) medical advice I was about to share and dove into the frozen dildo conversation. What I have learned over the years is that when the Internet gives you a topic, you lean in and take that gift and make it work. Over the next few weeks, that group grew exponentially, thanks a great deal to the open and honest conversations surrounding objects women were possibly willing to stick up their cooters to cool off. There were discussions around the pros and cons of jamming ordinary reusable ice cube sticks into your baby maker. You know the ones. They're perfectly designed to be frozen and then slid into water bottles—why not slide them into your hot box too? And I'd like to go ahead and offer my apologies to the makers of Fla-Vor-Ice Freezer Pops for the unspeakable things we contemplated doing with your fine product. In our defense, 2019 was a very hot summer.

I guess it should not have surprised me that the first topic to take off in Midlife Bites was vagina-related. I've always written about the vagina (yes, I know, it's really a vulva, but "vagina" has a better ring to it) and whenever any celebrity or wacko doctor is advising women to lift, tuck, or sew it, or better yet knit a fucking scarf from their vajeen, my readers send me the articles so I can publicly weigh in. I don't know why I thought Midlife Bites would be any different. Silly me.

As I write this, we're closing in on the first anniversary of Midlife Bites, and I asked the women in the group to share with me why they joined and why they stay. Here are just a few of the comments I received:

"I'm here because rivers of words have been written about men and their midlife crises, but women are just expected to put up with all the bullshit and changes (both internal and external) that affect us at this time of life. This group shines a light on a lot of the fuckery involved with being a woman of a certain age, and I don't feel so alone."   —Rachel

"This space is so authentic, supportive & safe . . . I've had the biggest laughs here and have always felt the care and concern of the group. Love the rawness and realness."   —Lisa

"I love this group. I have never really had girlfriends that are open enough to share their experiences and knowledge."   —Wendy

"I planned on getting a sporty orange car with a sunroof for my midlife crisis but instead I got a divorce . . . The support and encouragement I got from some of the great women here saved me on days I didn't think I could continue."

—Deanell

"I love this group because it makes me feel VALIDATED."

—Cheryl

"I came here because no one was talking about menopause! There was this great void I saw in the center of our lives filled with secrets that felt like they were supposed to be shameful and it pissed me off."

—Jennifer

"I use it like the What to Expect When Expecting book but for middle age, hormones, teenagers, chin hairs, swamp crotch, and aging parents."

—Janeen

"The menopause brought me here but the laughs, support, and non-judgmental advice is what keeps me here. I have found my tribe."

—Lisa

And of course:

"I've learned more about frozen dildos than I ever thought possible."

—Denise

JEN'S GEMS

You might think you're the only person interested in a topic, but I am positive there is a group for every hobby or interest you have. I don't care what you're looking for, there is an online group for everyone, and I encourage you to do some digging and find your people. For instance, a quick search revealed there is a group for owners of ferrets who live in Oklahoma. I also found a group of women entrepreneurs who own RVs and enjoy camping in the national parks. And I was even motivated to join a group for women over fifty who are interested in learning more about weight lifting, because osteoporosis and shit.

What Are You Even Doing
with Your Life?

Finding Your Purpose

I am asking you this question as your friend. Seriously, sometimes we need to sit ourselves down and ask ourselves the hard questions.

I met my friends Katie and Sophie for coffee one morning a few years back, and we'd barely sat down before Katie announced, "Well, that's it. I'm done being a mom now."

"What are you talking about?" I questioned.

"Ella goes to college in the fall," Katie said.

Sophie nodded sympathetically. "Ella's the youngest. Soon your nest will be empty."

Katie nodded. "Yeah, and I know what's next. They come home once or twice a year so I can do their laundry—"

"And raid the pantry," Sophie interrupted.

"They don't need a full-time mom anymore." Katie sighed.

"They need a laundromat and an ATM. Now that Michael's studying abroad, with the time change, he never calls anymore. He only texts us now. And even then it's just to ask us to put more money in his bank account."

"I bet your life feels a bit like it's over," Sophie said, biting into her scone.

How could she be so callous? "That's terrible, Katie," I said. "I'm so sorry."

"No! Don't be sad," Katie said. "It's okay. In some ways it's good. Jim and I will have our lives back again."

Sophie nodded wisely. "Keith and I have been on our own for three years now." Sophie suddenly stopped eating her scone and looked at me intently. "Prepare yourself, Jen. It's harder than you can imagine."

"You think you know, but you don't know," Katie said.

I gulped. "What's harder than I can imagine?"

Sophie shrugged. "All of it. Your relationship. There are no kids to act as a buffer anymore between you and the Hubs. After twenty-something years, you're suddenly together again and you're not sure if you have anything in common anymore."

"The loss of identity," Katie added. "Like, who am I now? Did I ever have hobbies that didn't include watching Michael play soccer and fundraising for Ella's marching band?"

"The silence in your house will be deafening," Sophie said.

"It's already so quiet! Ella hasn't officially left, but she's never home now that summer's started. You can't believe it. Even the dog misses her," Katie said.

"And the hole that's left in your heart," Sophie said quietly.

"It was so hard to send Michael off," Katie said. "Maybe Ella will be easier."

I could feel her sadness radiating across the table. They were right, I wasn't ready for this kind of pain. I still had four years left before Gomer left for college and I was already panicking. Was he ready to be on his own? Was I ready to let him go? Was I doing enough to prepare us both?

"And what about all that free time you have suddenly?" Sophie asked. "Your calendar is empty now that graduation is over. There's nothing to do until it's time to drop her off at her dorm in the fall."

"Quiet and free time actually sound kind of great," I said, hopefully.

"Yeah, until you're sitting all alone in your quiet house and you ask yourself: What have I done with my life?" Katie said.

"Do I have friends anymore?" Sophie added.

"Right? Most of my friends are Ella's friends' moms, and we really don't have that much in common," Katie continued.

Sophie nodded vigorously. "Yes! Just because we had kids with similar interests doesn't mean we should be friends."

"Exactly. I've been a mom for twenty-one years. I love being a mom, but I'm looking forward to being Katie again, not just Michael and Ella's mom," Katie said brightly, but I could see she was trying to fake a smile.

I suspected that that wasn't going to be as easy as she thought. As long as I'd known Katie, she'd never had a full-time job outside the home. She was the supermom who drove carpool every day and helped out in her kids' classrooms. She ran the PTA in elementary school, planned the eighth-grade graduation, and took over all the fundraising for the marching band in high school. Years ago I invited Katie to join a book club with me and she told me she didn't have time to read a book.

"I haven't read a book since Ella was born, Jen," Katie had said. "When would I read?"

Ummm . . . how about every time you're waiting for your insanely busy kids to get done with whatever activity they're doing?

As far as I could tell, Katie's whole life revolved around Michael and Ella. Sophie was the same way. In fact, Katie and Sophie met when their sons played soccer together in elementary school. They bonded over their shared love of elaborate displays of healthful team snacks. I met them both when I volunteered at church, and I liked them immediately because even though they were high overachievers, they owned that shit and were really relatable when you got past their ridiculous but delicious snacks. Plus, on the rare occasion I want to throw a party, I know I can count on Katie and Sophie to make it uber extra. I'm still not sure why they keep *me* around, maybe it's pity. They probably think I'm the ultimate fixer-upper project.

"You'll need a new purpose, Katie," Sophie said.

I saw Katie's smile falter.

For a fraction of a second I felt superior to Katie and Sophie. I had a purpose! This was one area in which I felt like I was winning as compared to Katie. I was never a stay-at-home mom who volunteered for every committee and party and drove carpool every other night. I'd had a full-time career since before Gomer was born. Yes, I was Gomer and Adolpha's mom, but I also had my own identity. I was Jen fucking Mann. I was "People I Want to Punch in the Throat." I was a *New York Times* bestselling author and an award-winning blogger. I entertained thousands of people every day. My kids were a huge part of my life, but my life didn't revolve around my kids. My life was robust and full!

But then I heard a little voice in the back of my mind: *Yeah, are you sure your life is that full? Do you have a purpose, or do you have a job? I think you just described a job. Lots of people have jobs, don't most people have more going on than a job?*

"Do you have a purpose, Sophie?" I asked, hesitantly. I waited, wondering if she'd confess that she, too, wasn't positive.

"I work with animals," Sophie said. "I volunteer at the no-kill shelter near my house. I love dogs. All my life I've had a dog. My dogs brought me so much happiness and now I can help them. Working there gives me the flexibility to travel with Keith or go see my kids."

"It gets you out of the house, I guess," I said.

Sophie looked at me intently. "No, Jen, it gives me a *purpose*. I'm doing something important. Everyone needs a sense of purpose. Otherwise, what's the point?"

None of the other women I knew talked about purpose the way Sophie did. They talked about their responsibilities and their commitments, but they didn't talk about their *purpose*. It was refreshing, but also a bit unnerving. Sophie can be a bit intense at times, but we all need that one intense friend to kick our ass.

I looked at Katie. "So what's your purpose going to be?"

Katie scoffed. "Hell if I know. But I better figure it out quick or else I'm going to be a mess." Katie understood that her life was going to change drastically and she needed to find something else to throw herself into.

"It's important," Sophie said. "Especially for your mental health, Katie. You won't be happy if you don't have a purpose."

"A purpose makes you happy?" I asked. I thought it was just something you did so you weren't bored.

"Of course," Sophie said. "The two are so closely related. That's why I work with dogs. Dogs bring me such joy. Yes, it's a job, and I have to show up several times a week, and it isn't glamorous or even fun always, but I am happy when I'm there."

I thought about what Sophie said. She was one of the happiest people I knew, and when I thought about it more, I realized that the happiest people I knew had purpose in their life. Without a purpose, we tend to drift through life rather than living it. Katie was happy right now because her purpose was caring for her kids, but in a few months all of that would be over. Katie had once told me she had postpartum depression, and all I could think about was her sliding back into a depression when Ella left home. "How do you know what your purpose is?" I exclaimed.

Sophie smiled. "A purpose can mean different things to different people. For instance, I know you well enough to know you wouldn't want to take care of dogs all day. And I wouldn't want the pressure to get up onstage and speak to groups or entertain people on the Internet."

"Wait. That's a purpose? I thought that was a job," I said.

Sophie laughed. "You're lucky. It's both!"

Phew! I was relieved. It's not like Sophie was an expert on purposes or anything, but it did feel better to hear her say that I had one.

We spent the rest of our time trying to help Katie discover her purpose. We had to ask the big questions. I even pulled up Pinterest and Instagram, because even though those inspomemes on the Internet are kind of cheesy, they're always being shared, because they work!

This is what we figured out:

Play to your strengths! Now is *not* the time to challenge

yourself by trying something batshit crazy new. Katie's a born leader. She's organized and she can motivate people to get shit done. She's always pitched in with big projects like PTA or Booster Club, because she knows she's great at managing projects with lots of moving parts. Katie's at her happiest when she's got a spreadsheet in front of her and she's ticking off the boxes with her red pen. Her kids' schools and sports clubs didn't need her skills anymore, but surely there were organizations out there that would love to put Katie to work!

"You could volunteer for a nonprofit or something. Like what Sophie's doing, but more managerial stuff. Organizing fundraisers, managing volunteers," I suggested.

She wrinkled her nose. "Honestly, I'd like to get paid now. In the past, it was nice to volunteer because I could still be flexible for the kids, but now we could use the money. Is that bad?"

"Absolutely not," Sophie said.

"I want a job, but I want it to be a job that gives me a sense of purpose," Katie said. "I don't want to just work somewhere for a paycheck."

Sophie and I nodded.

"That one's a bit tougher," Sophie said. "What gets you out of bed every morning?"

"My bladder," I joked.

Katie laughed. "Not much gets me out of bed, but gardening keeps me busy. I don't know what it is, but I love growing things. Flowers, herbs, vegetables. My watermelons are almost ready! And, you know me, I'm always giving away the excess because I grow so much. We couldn't use it all if we tried."

Sophie and I both had bags of zucchini sitting in front of us, which was very generous of Katie, but if I'm being honest, I really wanted a watermelon. Seriously, what am I going to do with squash?

Sometimes it can be difficult to see where your passion and your purpose can intersect. But it doesn't have to be that hard. You just need to figure out what kind of energy you have to put into this thing. Your purpose doesn't necessarily have to be your job or your side hustle, either. It might never bring you any cash. And that's okay. It's not about that. It's about giving you a focus, something to look forward to, something you're responsible for.

"Ooh! What if you worked at one of those local farm-to-table kind of places?" I said. "I mean, the job is a lot more than growing food. But those kinds of places are gaining popularity, and your organization and planning skills would be great for the business side, plus you could still get your hands dirty!"

"Or what about politics?" Sophie suggested. "You're very passionate about politics. You could knock on doors for a politician you support or maybe find a job at their campaign headquarters."

"Do you have any hobbies?" I asked.

Katie laughed. "I love knitting! Can I do something with that?"

I nodded. "I saw a story on the Internet about how knitting is an extremely therapeutic activity. You could start an ad-driven YouTube channel and teach people how to knit so they can lower their anxiety. And I'll be your first subscriber."

"Or start a knitting group that meets once a week or once a month or three times a year," Sophie said.

"Just join a knitting club for you. Have some great conversations while you make a kick-ass afghan!" I said.

"I wish I could do something with genealogy. I love tracing my roots. I'm pretty sure I'm descended from royalty," Sophie said.

"Yeah, well, I'm pretty sure I'm descended from the peasants who worked your land," I said.

After an hour or so, we had a good list for Katie to explore. Some were paying gigs that intersected with her passions, others channeled her hobbies. All of them were easily attainable and not one of them was what I'd call "If I won the lottery" ideas. I feel like a lot of times when celebrities or millionaires talk about their purpose, they're outlandish ideas that the rest of us can only achieve with a winning Powerball number.

The Hubs and I don't play the lottery very often, only the few times a year when the pot is so big it makes the news. We cross our fingers and spend a few bucks and then take the next several hours to discuss our Lottery Plan. What? You don't know what a Lottery Plan is? Okay, ours is like this:

- Will we take the lump sum or the yearly payout? *Lump sum, duh.*
- We'll have to pay X amount to taxes. *Gladly, we still have millions left.*
- We'll pay off all our bills, in this particular order. *Done, done, and done!*
- We'll put money away for the kids to go to college. *Grad school for both of them!*
- We'll give some money to family and friends. *No, you're probably not on our list.*
- We'll give away some money to charities we care about. *No, you're not a charity. You don't count.*
- And then we'll follow our bliss.

The Hubs will definitely do something businessy. He'll invest in his own business as well as other businesses, that sort of thing. He'll be that philanthropic business guy around town.

I'll still write, but I'll write with absolutely no pressure. I won't have to worry about writing books that will sell. I can finally write that novel that's been kicking around in my brain for years. It's a dystopian time-traveling space cowboy vampire book loosely based on the House of Tudor. I'm pretty sure I'm the only person in the world (besides Queen Katie) who wants to read that book, so only a lottery winner could afford to write it.

The fact is that the chances of any of us winning the lottery are very low, but it's fun to dream, right?

So, what would you do?

I bet you're saying, "I don't know."

But that's not true. You know. Or at least your gut knows. No, those aren't hunger pains. That's your gut talking to you. What's it saying? There's a little voice inside you that knows what you'd do, but you're too afraid to say it out loud. Maybe it's too risky. Maybe it's too expensive. Or maybe it's too time-consuming. Maybe it seems silly. It doesn't matter, you can still say it. Go on, try it. No one's listening.

When I asked my community what they'd do with their lottery winnings, I received hundreds of answers. Many wanted to pay off all their debt (and even the debt of their friends and loved ones) and retire. Several wanted to travel and see the world. A few wanted to use the money to help others who were in greater need than they were. One even wanted to create a scholarship in her cat's name. You do you, my cat-loving friend.

I don't think I worded my question properly, because many

really never got to the part about what they'd do once they were debt-free. Everyone was so focused on getting that medical bill paid off or covering their kids' college expenses, they didn't get to the "following their bliss" part.

So I reworded my question and tried again. Some of my friends had risky ideas like starting huge nonprofits or opening a chain of restaurants, but many of the answers I received were about moving to a new place, traveling more, reading more, spending time helping people and animals—all fairly low-risk ideas that didn't require the lottery and could benefit their and others' lives.

When you can't pinpoint your purpose, asking this question can point you in the right direction. Your answer might feel scary, but really it's exactly what you need in order to feel alive and to help you find your bliss. What are you waiting for? You're getting older, and you're not getting any happier. Take that chance!

Hang on, no one's telling you to sell all your shit and move into a yurt in the wilds of Maine and make baskets out of your hair. Unless that's what you'd do if you didn't need money! Even then, I'm not sure that's a great idea. That's really a Lottery Plan, like my novel.

Instead, start a bit smaller. Maybe move to Maine, or just plan a visit. Or if those steps are too big even, start making baskets out of your hair in your free time. Baby steps are still steps. Take them.

I haven't written my genre-bending opus yet, but I did take the plunge and quit my day job a few years ago and started writing full time. I never felt more terrified and happy, all at the same time. It was scary to think that I had to make money writing, but it was so exciting to finally be doing exactly what I wanted. Something that truly inspired me.

What would you do if you knew you couldn't fail? Seriously. What would you do? Think about it.

My husband is really good at this one. Whether I like it or not, he never allows himself to think about failure. He's all about the energy he puts out there in the universe. He believes wholeheartedly that what you put out there is what you get back. He's never been afraid to try something new. He's had probably five different careers since I've known him (some of them were by choice, some by circumstance). He's walked away from jobs that didn't suit him, and he's been laid off from jobs, but he was never worried (even though I was). He knew he'd land on his feet somehow. He never feels intimidated by subject matter, because he believes he can teach himself everything he needs to know. "Nobody woke up with all the knowledge in their head," he says. "They had to learn it, so anyone can learn it." He shares all of himself with the people he cares about. He has as much belief in them as he does in himself.

I don't know what he thinks his purpose is, but I know what I think it is: to enable others to succeed. He believes everyone has greatness inside them, it just needs to be found and tapped. He helps people find their inner confidence and motivates them to achieve their dreams. He's never met a person he didn't want to help.

A few years ago I received an email from an old boyfriend, a guy I dated briefly before the Hubs. He wrote me a message to say he was surprised to come across my book at the bookstore and even more surprised when he googled me and found out what I'd accomplished since we saw each other last. "You're a rock star!" he wrote. He went on to say that he was sorry our relationship hadn't worked out and that he wondered what it would be like to be married to a "rock star."

I never replied to his email. Partly because it was super-strange to hear from him after so many years (WTF, dude?) and partly because my response would have been: "Dear Old Boyfriend, I probably wouldn't be a 'rock star' if I was married to you."

I don't mean that in an unkind way. I just mean that without my husband and his driving purpose of pushing me and in-spiring me to follow my dreams, I probably wouldn't have books on the shelves at the store. I might not have my thriving online platform. I definitely wouldn't have the confidence to try new things without the fear of failure. That's not to say I don't think I'm talented on my own, but before I met the Hubs, I did have a tendency to underestimate my potential. And I never had a boyfriend who motivated me the way he did. Over the years he has helped me gain confidence and see that I am limitless. When I forget, he is the one who reminds me that failure is just part of learning, that fear is what holds me back from my purpose.

If you had asked five-year-old me "What would you do if you knew you couldn't fail?"

Five-year-old me would have said "Write books."

It would be easy to think that's my purpose, but it's not. That's not what I'm here for. My purpose has always been to entertain people and to create a community where women felt they belonged.

Listening to Sophie talk about dogs made me realize she knows the secret, but so many middle-aged women don't. Or if we did know the secret once, we've forgotten it. We've become so bogged down in our work, in our relationships, and in our never-ending to-do lists that we've lost sight of our purpose.

I understood that I'd lost sight of my own purpose over the last few years. I'd been drifting, and that's one of the reasons why I was feeling so overwhelmed. I'd allowed my purpose to turn into a J-O-B and that was one of the reasons why I was so unhappy. I needed to get back to when my purpose wasn't just tied to a paycheck. I needed to start waking up every day with my purpose as my priority. It needed to be my reason to get out of bed again.

Keep in mind that purposes can change and evolve over time, but one thing is for certain, you must always have one. Without it—your North Star, your why, whatever you want to call it—you are destined to drift.

But don't get hung up on thinking you have to find your *one* thing. That's crazy. So many things propel me to always be moving forward. I am a wife, a mother, a friend, a writer, a publisher, a blogger, a humorist, an influencer (barf, I hate that word), a motivator, a lover of swear words, a despiser of pants. And I give great fucking hugs.

JEN'S GEMS

You still don't know your purpose? It's okay. Let's figure this out together. Make a list of all the things that motivate and inspire you. What's on that list? Anything good? Try asking your friends what their purposes are. Maybe their answers can guide you. Don't overthink it. Look at that list again. It's there. Your purpose doesn't have to be something expensive or time-consuming. Here are just a few of the answers I received that are easy and could be done today: Spend time with the elderly, teach English as a second language, start a garden, coach youth sports, express yourself through music or art.

Make Some Fucking Friends

Putting Yourself Out There

I have a confession to make and I'm not going to sugarcoat it. I'm just going to go ahead and say it. I have a hard time finding friends, and I'm lonely because of it.

Phew. That was kind of tough, wasn't it?

But it needed to be said, because I know I'm not the only woman who feels this way.

I see it all the time. It is easily the number one complaint I hear from the women I encounter IRL and on my social media platform. We all know now what the first question was that took off and started a huge conversation in the Midlife Bites group (frozen dildos). But what I really want to talk about is the *second* question that produced a lot of good discussion. It was "How do you find friends in midlife?"

I read through all of the responses, hoping for some good

advice, but instead I found so much anguish in the comment thread. I was genuinely surprised to see the ways that many women from many different backgrounds responded to the question. It didn't matter what they looked like, where they lived, who they lived with, or what their bank account looked like. They all shared an overwhelming sense of loneliness. Every single one of these women craved meaningful friendships, same as me. I could see that the feelings of isolation, anxiety, and apathy were prevalent with so many of them, ultimately sabotaging them from forming true connections with other people. Which then all compounded into a perfect storm that made the women feel even lonelier and even more desperate for real friendship.

I found this especially troubling because, seriously, it shouldn't be that hard to make a friend. We were able to do it easily enough when we were kids. What had changed?

By the way, when I say "friend" or "friendship," I'm not talking about casual acquaintances. We're not hermits or trolls living alone under a bridge. Of course we interact with people most every day—co-workers, moms on the pickup line, the deli counter guy. I'm talking about *true* friendships where we can be one hundred percent ourselves without fear of judgment. That is the unicorn that so many of us are in search of.

I don't know about you, but there was a time when I was incredibly envious of the BFF cliques I encountered in my daily life, even though I would never admit it to them or to myself. I saw groups of women from my neighborhood going for coffee or wine together. I followed their #girlstrip online and wondered what I had to do to be invited into their inner sanctum. I didn't even need to go to Belize with them. I would have been happy to be invited to a book club or a Scentsy party or even a fucking running club. Actually, that's not true, I hate running. But I was hungry for someone I could connect with on a deeper level. I was desperate to find someone I could tell the truth to when I was asked "How are you, Jen?"

A couple of years ago my car broke down on the highway. I was able to pull off onto the shoulder, but I still felt unsafe. Cars and trucks were whizzing dangerously close to me, and my car shook every time they passed. I was a few yards from a homemade memorial someone had made for a stranded motorist who'd been killed in a hit-and-run at that very spot. I shuddered. I wanted to get the fuck out of there. I was prepared to abandon the car and call for a tow truck from home. I sat there for a minute wondering who I could call to come and pick me up. My husband was out of town. My parents were out of town. Even my brother and his family were out of town. None of my usual suspects were around. I'm lucky that I have my family so close. I've never had anyone but family babysit my kids or bring me a meal when I was sick. Because I've always been able to rely on my family, I didn't have any of those kinds of friends who can come and pick you up on the side of the highway in the middle of a weekday in my phone. I scrolled through the names in my contacts list and found myself thinking, "Hmm. No, not Stephanie, we're not that close, I wouldn't want to bother her," or "Frank? Oh wait, I think that's my dentist. That reminds me, I need to make an appointment for a cleaning," or "Nora's mom. Shit, what's her first name? I can't call her Nora's mom. Never mind, I think she moved away." I was in tears when I finally called the Hubs. I'm not sure what I was more upset about, the fact that my car was disabled and I was scared, or the fact that I had no friends I could call on for help.

When the Hubs said, "What exactly do you think I can do right now from fifteen hundred miles away?" I hung up on him and googled tow services. If I wanted to make you feel good about this story, I'd lie to you and tell you the tow truck driver was a woman named Kathleen and mine was her last call of the day so she suggested we grab a drink and discuss books and overthrowing the patriarchy and we're now best friends who vacation in Belize together.

Nope.

That's not what happened. The tow truck driver's number is in my phone now, and even though he'll be my first call next time I'm on the side of the road, he is definitely not a friend.

Of course, I'd like to blame my lack of friends on this whole midlife thing, but that wouldn't be fair. To be honest, I've always had a hard time making friends. As a kid I was painfully shy, and my family moved around a lot. Just when I'd get up the nerve to invite someone over to my house, it was time to pack up and move again. When I finally did muster the confidence to befriend someone, it usually ended badly. Like teen movie bad. I've been uninvited to birthday parties, I've been the recipient of ransom-note-looking hate mail shoved into my locker, I've been tormented by boys about my appearance, and once I was even the pet project of a group of popular mean girls. They adopted me and brought me into their fold only to literally abandon me as a joke at a high school football game and I had to find my way home after being stranded. It was an away game and I was new in town, so I had no clue where I was. Cellphones didn't exist yet, so I had to find a payphone and hunt down the name of the school so my dad could use the Yellow Pages to find me. The only positive thing I can say about my high school experience is I didn't get a bucket of pig blood dumped on me, nor did I burn down the place with my nonexistent telekinetic powers (although I may have tried). Once I made it home from the football game, I pretty much gave up trying to make friends.

In my mind it wasn't worth the hassle or the heartache. It was easier to pretend I didn't want to belong and reject people before they could reject me. To keep people at bay, I hid behind a wall of witty zingers and withering facial expressions. This approach stuck with me for a long time. It saved my feelings and added to the sarcastic loner persona I had spent years cultivating.

It wasn't until the dawn of the Internet age that I finally started to find my people—people who I could actually connect with and who understood me. A lot of people I know in real life think it's weird that most of my closest friends live in the computer, but I think it's weird that society thinks I should be friends with Laura just because she randomly bought the house next door to me. At least on the Internet I can find people who have the same passions, values, and interests as me. (No, Laura, the fact that we were both drawn to the Westerfield II floor plan doesn't count as a common interest.)

I joined the Internet in the early nineties. I landed my first job, and my first big splurge was a computer.

I bought a computer because I had plans to write the Great American Novel. I figured once I had the computer all I needed were a teakettle and a cat and I'd be all set. How hard could it be?

I opened up the box and right on top was a shiny disc that immediately caught my eye. I pulled it out and examined it. "AOL?" I read aloud. "What's that?"

Looking back now, I realize I probably should have left that disc alone and just started writing. I might have actually written the Great American Novel and won a Nobel Prize or something. But I couldn't resist the temptation. I had to know what AOL was. It would be the first time (but certainly not the last time) something shiny and/or the Internet would distract me from my writing.

I logged on to AOL and immediately felt at home. I didn't have to be Jen Mann, the awkward, chunky girl in the corner with the weird opinions and dark sense of humor. I could conceal my identity behind a screen name and showcase only the parts of myself I wanted to reveal while staying relatively anonymous. In those days many of us didn't have the technology to add a picture to our profile, so I didn't have the additional worry of being judged by my looks. I could join chat rooms dedicated to discussions on topics important to me. Like dissecting Rachel's hairdo in the latest episode of *Friends*, lamenting with fellow wannabe writers over our lack of time to write (yes, I can see the irony now, but at the time we totally blamed our "real" jobs for sucking up our writing time, not chatting on AOL for hours on end), and heated arguments about whether Ewoks were cuddly, deadly, or a combination of both (it's becoming clearer why I don't have any friends, isn't it?).

Anyhoo, one day I was deep in a controversial conversation about how can Imperial stormtroopers be considered such elite fighters when they're such horrible shots when I received a private message from a dude on the other side of the country weighing in with his opinion.

That was the first time the Internet changed my life and helped me find a best friend. Several years later, that dude would become the Hubs.

We struck up an online friendship, and he was one of the first people I let see the "real" me. It was easy because I thought we'd never meet in real life. He was in New York City and I was in Kansas City. What were the odds? I didn't censor myself. I let my nerdiness run wild. I put my raunchy sense of humor out there on full display. And I shared my strong opinions with abandon, on everything from politics to books to people's shitty driving skills. In some ways I was more myself than I'd ever been, because I felt I could be freer online than I could be in person.

Looking back on it now, I realize that if the Hubs and I had met at a party, I'm not sure we would ever have spoken to each other. We're both fairly shy and reserved in large groups and we take a while to "warm" up. Plus, neither one of us would have had the guts to approach the other and talk about *Star Wars* at a party full of grown-ass adults. But online we were a perfect match. Both of us could be our true selves, and we found each other interesting.

So interesting, in fact, that a couple years later I moved to New York City to be closer to him.

After I got there I found myself once again friendless. The Hubs would have been perfectly content for it to always be just the two of us, but I craved a little more human interaction. Not much, just a friend or two. It took me a while to land a job, and with him working full time, I was alone a lot. I had struggled with meeting friends as a kid, but I sucked at meeting people as an adult. I was unemployed, childless, petless, and living by myself, so there weren't a lot of opportunities to meet new friends. And the Hubs wasn't much help. He had only a handful of friends himself, and I had nothing in common with them.

Finally, after growing sick of listening to me whine, the Hubs suggested I join a group.

"What kind of group?" I complained, already dreading the idea of putting on pants and leaving my apartment.

"Something that interests you," he offered, helpfully.

"Ugh," I groaned. In my opinion, I'd found that most people's "interests" were things that did not appeal to me. Things like scrapbooking, biking, gardening, parenting, that sort of thing.

He sighed. "I can think of at least one thing that interests you," he said, gesturing toward my overflowing bookshelves. "What about joining a book club?"

"Book clubs are for old ladies," I groaned. "My *mom* belongs to a book club."

"You're not even trying, Jen," the Hubs scowled. "Do you want friends or not?"

I considered his question. I was lonely and I did need someone else to gripe to or else I was going to chase off the one person I really cared about. Maybe a book club wouldn't be *so* terrible. Sure, only "women of a certain age" joined book clubs, but maybe I would make a friend at book club? A middle-aged friend was still a friend, right? "Fine," I said. "But where would I even find this group?"

He smiled and sat down at my computer. "The same place you met me: the Internet." With a few keystrokes he found what he was looking for. "Here you go!"

The next day I tried to talk myself out of showering, getting dressed, and walking eight blocks to a restaurant to meet a bunch of strange women from the Internet who loved books as much as I did. I knew that even if we had nothing in common and couldn't think of a thing to talk about, we could talk about books. And yet I still wasn't convinced I should go.

Yes, I was lonely, and yes, I needed a friend, but was I *that* lonely? Was I really prepared to meet a bunch of crazy strangers from the Internet? And then I reminded myself I'd recently moved across the country to date a crazy stranger I'd met on the Internet. Clearly, my standards were not very high.

I finally put on cleanish pants and dragged myself down the street with the hope of making a new friend.

Okay, if I'm being honest, it wasn't exactly the hope of meeting a new friend that motivated me. It was the lack of food in my fridge and the siren song of the mozzarella sticks that I knew would be waiting for me at the restaurant even if a friend wasn't.

I arrived at the restaurant and immediately felt insecure walking in alone. "Can I help you?" the hostess asked.

I looked around. The restaurant was teeming with couples gazing lovingly into each other's eyes, messy families with obnoxious children (I hated kids in those days because I didn't understand yet how exhausted those mothers were), and happy groups of co-workers enjoying drink specials near the bar (I've never understood people who want to hang out together after work, I barely want to work with you, I definitely don't want to drink with you). I wanted to turn around and walk out. Nope—I wanted to *run* the eight blocks back to my apartment and strip off my bra in the front hall of my apartment.

"Umm," I hesitated. *Be brave!* I thought.

"Are you meeting someone?" the hostess asked.

"Umm." I felt my heart quicken and my mouth go dry.

I'm not this brave, I thought. *Well, yes, you are too brave. Also, mozzarella sticks, dummy!*

"Maybe a group?" the hostess offered, kindly.

I nodded. "A book club," I said.

The hostess smiled and nodded. "They're waiting for you in the back room."

Within a few months of splitting an order of mozzarella sticks and scrutinizing the significance of an author's choice of blue drapes in the parlor, I'd found a full-time job and made some friends at work, too, but my book club remained special to me. They were my first grown-up friends, and they came at just the right time in my life. We held weekly "official" meet-ups, but several of us bonded and would hang out outside the normal schedule. They made me feel included and instantly became my tribe. We shared a common interest, which really did help to facilitate a real friendship or two.

Over the years, the Internet has continued to play an important role in helping me find friends. After several years of living in New York City, the Hubs and I decided to move back to Kansas and start a family. Motherhood was the toughest job I'd ever had, and no matter how hard the Hubs tried, he couldn't understand my mood swings or help me with my bleeding nipples. Once again I found myself turning to the Internet to find a group to join.

I found an online mothers' group and attended an in-person meeting with the local chapter. I'd like to say the first group I joined had the same magic as my book club, but it didn't. If you've had a child, then you know the kind of judgment and nonsense that go along with parenting groups. This group was no different. Playgroups can be hard. The fact that we had children born the same year in the same town brought us together, but it didn't necessarily mean we'd find anything else to bond over. But I didn't give up. I knew there was a group for me out there, I just had to keep looking. It took me a few more tries before I finally found a mothers' group I could work with. This group wasn't perfect either, but that was a good lesson for me, actually.

There was a lot of pressure to fit in with the other new moms. I needed to host elaborate playdates, read the right parenting books, get my kids into the finest preschools, and sign them up for the best extracurriculars, all while looking fit and fabulous. I didn't quit, though, because now I had Gomer to think of. I worked from home and Gomer spent all day with me. I'd joined the group hoping I'd make a friend or two, but I'd really joined so *Gomer* could make friends. I had to stay for him! I tried to keep up with the other moms, but I was unsuccessful and it made me feel despondent.

I realized that for years I'd been trying to fit my square peg into every group's round hole. I'm not everyone's cup of tea, and as I aged into my midthirties, I realized that I was tired of trying to please everyone. I was tired of keeping my head down and my mouth shut. I was tired of taking my personality down a notch and pretending I was someone I wasn't just so I could go with the flow or not cause waves or fit in or whatever I was trying to do. Instead of changing, I decided I'd rather be myself and attract the few people who liked me for me.

I started with that mothers' group. I went to work and I shaped it into what *I* wanted. I did this by inviting others to join the group. I figured the more members we had, the better chance I had of meeting people like me.

I began by taking on a leadership role. I wasn't crazy about some of the leaders, so I decided to run for an open position on the board. (Yeah, this playgroup had a board of directors. I know, don't get me started on that shit.) I worked to change that group from the inside out. Yes, I wanted to make new friends, but I also wanted other new moms out there to feel less alone. Even though the group wasn't perfect, it was still a godsend for me. I made a few close friends I couldn't imagine trying to navigate the murky waters of first-time motherhood without.

It was the first time I'd put myself out there and really taken charge of something. I'd been a member of a number of groups before then, but I'd never been a part of the leadership. I decided I liked it. Of course I did. I'm a bossy person. That's okay, I own it. If you want something done right, you need to do it yourself.

After a few years, our kids started going off to different schools, some of the women moved away or got full-time jobs, and those friendships fizzled. I felt the familiar ache of loneliness start to creep back in. This time there wasn't a group to join. Believe me, I tried. I searched and searched the Internet, but everything out there was designed to socialize the kids, not the moms. My kids played sports and participated in afterschool activities, but I didn't really bond with the other moms on the sidelines. I couldn't get into the rah-rah or the hypercompetitive atmosphere around pee-wee soccer. They were eight years old, they weren't professional athletes, for fuck's sake.

I also struggled to fit in with the moms, because there wasn't an easy category for me. I was a real estate agent and I worked from home so I could save on expenses and spend time with my family. I didn't quite fit in with the stay-at-home moms, and since I didn't put on pants and go to a legit office every day, I didn't fit in with the working moms. I was in a no-mom's-land where everyone let me know my situation was abnormal and probably bad for my children. The stay-at-home moms hinted that my job forced me to neglect my kids, and the working moms insinuated it wasn't really "working" if you could do it in your jammies.

My lack of friends started to affect my marriage. I was irritable and stressed because I had no one to bitch to other than the Hubs. I looked at book clubs, but I hadn't had time to read a book since Gomer was born. With the playgroup moms I had an outlet to vent or commiserate about the struggles of parenting and husbands, but it would be weird to show up for a playgroup without a baby.

I needed a friend who would listen. I've found that women don't necessarily want to have their problems solved; they do, however, want to be heard. That's one major complaint I have about the Hubs. I had to teach him early on that I just wanted to bitch and moan. I didn't want actual solutions or what he thought was the right way to go about solving the problem. And I wanted to him to lie to me a little. I wanted to hear that I was right, or at least that my outrage was righteous. I wanted him to nod along and say "That sucks" and "Fuck that guy!" I didn't want him to say "Now, Jen, you do realize you aren't blameless here, right?" Every time he did that, we would fight.

That's when I started the "People I Want to Punch in the Throat" blog.

Even though I was miserable, a lot of what I wrote was still funny. It was sarcastic and biting and witty. I've decided the only thing that's kept me sane all these years is my sense of humor. Yeah, I can get really pissed off really fast, but I can also take a step back and see the humor in just about any situation.

Life is hard. You're going to laugh or cry, so you might as well laugh. By being my true authentic self, I was able to connect with people, draw them to me, and forge real friendships.

When the blog went viral and I decided to try to make a career out of this writing thing, I started spending a lot more time online than I ever had before. A lot had changed since my AOL days! I didn't realize that there were so many different super-niche groups you could join. I went on a joining frenzy. I joined a Midwest moms blogging group. I joined a Jane Austen fan group that gets together for brunch every year on her birthday. I joined a local networking group that was exclusively for work-at-home moms. I also joined a fuck ton of crafting groups, because my deepest, darkest secret is how much I love a sizzling hot glue gun. If the snarky blog hadn't taken off, I'd be making holiday wreaths and hairbows for babies right now.

As much as I wanted to, I couldn't just hang out online all day. I had to actually leave my house and meet new people, and that was where it got a bit harder. First, I had to get over my fear of being the initiator. I used to get really hung up on how many times I invited a friend to do something versus how many times she invited me to do something. It's petty and silly to get caught up in that nonsense. As I talk to more women, I discover that there's a lot of fear of rejection out there, and when you combine it with the overwhelming sense of apathy a lot of women have, it makes total sense that you aren't being invited places. You have to take that first step and encourage your friend to join you on an adventure.

And don't get me started on the exhaustive process of making and keeping friends. I can relate to the overwhelming decision making that goes into choosing the right pants to wear to a happy hour with the ladies. I also worried about the judgment that comes with friends. Let's face it, women talk shit about one another. All the time. I don't care how close you and your bestie are, at some point she's made a snide remark behind your back. And that really sucks. But if you're being honest, you've made a snide remark about her too.

So, as I matured, I made this big deal that I wouldn't say shit behind my friends' backs anymore. I would be that brutally honest friend who tells them when their ass looks big in a pair of jeans, or that their parenting strategies suck, or that their husband is a tool. God, it's tough to be my friend, and I'm grateful for the four or so of you who have stuck with me.

I also had to come to terms with the kind of friend I am. Frankly, I am a bad friend. I can go days, even weeks, without checking in. I can get so wrapped up in my own life that I forget about my friendships. I've been working super-hard on being a better friend. I used to hate to text. I thought texting was dumb and laborious. Just call me and let's talk so I don't have to sit here with cramped thumbs! Plus, there was the added bonus of paralyzing overanalysis of every text message sent and received with new friends. *What did she mean by "K"? Like, is she mad or just really busy? Maybe that's a butt-dial and she didn't even mean to reply because she hates me now and is ghosting me. That's it. I'm done texting her. Arrgghh.* But over time I realized that a lot of people prefer a quick text check-in. So I started texting. And I learned very fast that it's an easy way to keep in touch with people and keep your connection. It doesn't take nearly as much effort as I thought it would, and I've fully embraced texting nothing but TikTok videos all day to some friends and completely inappropriate memes to others.

What I'm trying to tell you is that there is no magic bullet for finding friends. The secret is putting yourself out there. You have to be open to trying new things, pushing your comfort zone. Don't be afraid to make the first move. Take chances—be bold and brave. Yes, you'll probably meet some assholes. But you'll also meet some people who will tell you that you need a better bra and send you videos of dogs at the spa.

JEN'S GEMS

Listen, sometimes you have to be the one to reach out first. You can't sit at home and hope someone thinks of you. It doesn't work that way. If you meet someone you connect with, take a chance and initiate the relationship. Reach out digitally or by phone, or even in person. If they don't take you up on it, who cares? Try someone else. And once you do make that friend, you can't keep score. We're all going through our own shit and we need to give one another some grace instead of instantly assuming the worst. If you always keep the lines of communication open and let your friend know when you feel left out or unsure of where you stand, it's easier to get back on track. Communicating with new friends can be hard. When in doubt, text them a hilarious meme. It works every time.

Is That a Hair on My Nipple? And Other Things I Never Thought I'd Ask

Learning and Accepting Your Changing Body

> Age is an issue of mind over matter. If you don't mind, it doesn't matter.
>
> —Attributed to Mark Twain

I don't get my hair done as often as I should. I work from home and rarely leave the house, plus the Hubs is too cheap to encourage me to spend hundreds of dollars on my hair just so it looks good for him. So I only get it done when I know I'm going to attend a book signing or I've been hired to speak in front of a group. In between events, I let it do its thing, and then a few weeks before I'm scheduled to depart, I'll get an appointment with my stylist, Sarah, and she whips me into shape.

I've never embraced my natural color. I don't even remember what it looks like except that it's boring. I've dyed my hair assorted shades of red since seventh grade because it's a fun color. But when I turned forty, Sarah (who is a good ten years younger than me) suggested ever so gently, "Hey, Jen, have you ever thought about going blond?"

"Blond?" I scoffed. "I don't do blond. I'm a redhead."

Sarah squirmed. "Yeah, it's just that, when you go red, the color . . . uh . . . it grows out . . . a bit faster than when it's blond."

That made no sense to me. How could my hair grow faster or slower depending upon the color? "What do you mean? Red hair grows faster than blond?"

"Yeah, kind of," Sarah stammered. "It's just that, well, when we first started dyeing your hair red years ago your natural color was all brown and when it grew out, it wasn't so noticeable because it sort of blended with the red, since you have . . . well, you *had* reddish-brown highlights naturally. And now . . ."

"And now, what?" I demanded, looking closer at my hair in the mirror.

"Well, now . . . um . . . a lot of my clients who are older—"

"Older?" I interrupted her. "I'm an *older* client now?" I glared at Sarah.

"Um . . . just, you know, a little older. Just a *little*, Jen."

"Uh-huh."

"Well, my clients who are . . . um . . . who have more . . . um . . . who have *less* of their natural color now, they prefer to go blond, because when the blond grows out it blends with their . . . *new* natural color?"

What the fuck was she saying? *My new natural color?* My natural color is and always will be brown!

"What the hell are you trying to say?" I demanded. Sarah and I had known each other for years and I was irritated she was being so evasive with me. What was she getting at? It was like she was afraid to tell me something. And then realization dawned on me. My *new* natural color!

"Are you trying to tell me I'm *gray*? Are you saying my hair is *gray*? That my *new* natural color is *gray*?" Sarah stayed silent, so I kept going. "And when my auburn hair grows out, my natural color isn't brown anymore and the gray roots stand out, but with blond the gray roots are better camouflaged and thus I should be blond?"

The middle-aged stylist at the station next to us leaned over. "That's exactly what she's saying. You're too old for red. It's time for blond, baby. Why do you think all the older ladies have blond hair? Plus, your skin will look brighter, your eyes will pop. It will better all around. Not so severe." She nodded and then frowned and peered closely at my face. "Also, it's way past time to start waxing that lip. It's just getting darker instead of gray." She gathered up a pile of dirty towels and sauntered off toward the laundry room without even so much as an apology for dropping such a big-ass truth bomb on me.

"Damn," I said. "That was so fucking harsh for someone who doesn't even know me. Can you imagine what she says to her friends?"

Sarah shrugged. "Yeah, Miriam can be a lot to handle sometimes. She lost her filter a while ago. But she's not wrong. That lip could use some attention."

And so that's when I started dyeing my hair blond and getting my lip waxed on a semiregular basis.

When midlife hit some years ago, I went from being someone who barely glanced in the mirror before leaving the house to someone obsessed with every little detail of her face and body. My "laugh lines" were no longer disappearing, but my eyebrows were. I know I had eyebrows when I went to bed one night, and when I woke up the next morning, they were gone.

I lost the hair from my eyebrows, but then I had hair sprouting out of unusual spots: my ears, my chin, even my fucking nipple.

And my breasts! Oh my god, my breasts! I don't have many good qualities, but those breasts used to be my shining glory. Now they were no longer symmetrical. One was decidedly longer than the other. Yeah, I said longer, not bigger. They now both resemble two loaves of French bread racing toward my waist, one just a bit closer to winning than the other (it's the one without the hairy nipple, in case you were wondering). To still look halfway decent they require bras that consist mostly of industrial-grade reinforced wiring covered by a swatch of fabric and that run in the ballpark of no less than a hundred bucks apiece. Quite an effort.

Please don't ask about my nether regions. I could have swamp crotch on Monday and the Mojave Desert on Tuesday. I just try and keep it neat and as pleasant as I can for visitors.

I've never been a skinny girl. I'm more of an "hourglass" type. As I've aged, the hourglass has spread into more of a pear, and now I'm well on my way to a goddamn apple. The ironic part is that I'm actually moving more and eating less than ever before, and my middle-aged body is like, "Ha ha, you ate a salad. Yeah, that used to work. Not anymore. Fuck you."

Damn. How do hot chicks do this? How do they age? I wondered. *I'm not even high maintenance, and this fucking sucks!*

I was never a hot chick. Not even close. I was always the funny girl (looks and personality). I was every guy's friend but no one's girlfriend. I was never a hot chick, and yet here I was freaking out about my changing body. Imagine how fucked up

I'd be if I'd always been gorgeous and now I suddenly had a wattle?

I found myself thinking about other procedures I needed done. Dyeing my hair and waxing my lip weren't enough anymore. I heard women whispering about eyelash extensions, microblading, boob jobs, eyelifts, fillers, liposuction, vaginal rejuvenation, and more.

And I knew I wasn't the only one feeling this way. There's a reason why the aesthetic industry is worth $53 billion! Women are bombarded daily—hourly—with all this shit. There are a million ways to make us look younger and better. We're told that we need to pluck, wax, lift, and tuck everything on our bodies or else society will find us unworthy and unappealing. In addition to a wrinkle-free face, we need longer eyelashes, plumper lips, rounder booties, lifted boobies, trained waists, hairless bodies, and rejuvenated vaginas. And don't even get me started on the elixirs, tonics, and snake oils that promise to deliver everything from hair as thick as an actual pony's tail to the mind of a physicist to the sex life of a porn star to the energy of a long-distance runner. The medical industry is cashing in on our vanity and our fear of aging. And they're turning it into a party. I was recently invited to a Botox party. It's like a Tupperware party, except everyone pays to get an injection between their eyes instead of plastic containers that burp. I declined. I like frowning. It's my favorite expression.

And it's not just women my age or older who are buying into this madness. I have a friend who is a generation younger than me and she's already shelling out thousands of dollars every year to "combat" aging and keep it at bay. Her doctors and aestheticians have convinced her that the younger she starts this shit, the better it will be for her when she hits middle age—in fifteen fucking years.

Oh, come on! Men don't have this kind of pressure! They get to age however they want. They go gray, they go bald, they grow guts. Men don't give a fuck about any of it. Their backs are hairy, their feet are like sandpaper. I've seen earwax literally pop out of my husband's ear at the dinner table. I would *die* if that happened to me, but he just picked it up, examined it, and gave a sniff before he tossed it into the trash and said, "Meh. It happens sometimes."

Hell, "Dad Bod" is a real thing women lust after! Where are the Internet memes and Instagram accounts dedicated to the hotness of schlumpy middle-aged women?

I realized all this worrying about aging was just making me age faster. I had to calm the fuck down and figure out what I was going to do. I was forty-seven and staring straight at a crossroads. I had to choose how I was going to age.

I found that women have only a few choices:

1. Fight it to the death

You have to be really rich with a lot of free time and a ton of self-control if you're going to take this path. It is not for the weak. You're going to need a fleet of paid helpers and experts plus an iron will.

I know women who spend their entire day with personal trainers, nutrition coaches, aestheticians, dermatologists, cosmetic dermatologists, cosmetic dentists, plastic surgeons, hair stylists, makeup artists, personal stylists, and wellness coaches, all of them dedicated to the fight against Time. When these women are not getting poked, scraped, measured, straightened, or toned, they're aligning their chakras and getting direction from their spirit guides.

These women are running on five hours of sleep, protein shakes, hashtags, and sheer determination. They treat anti-aging like it's their goddamn job and they're going to win employee of the year. They refuse to age, and when they die, their family had better send them to their grave with their roots touched up and a fresh spray tan or they will haunt them for all of eternity!

This was not the path for me. While I admired the dedication of these women, I knew I'd fail terribly. Besides the fact that I couldn't afford any of this shit, my will is more akin to Jell-O than iron, and waking up before the sun rises so I can do anything except pee sounds like hell on earth to me.

2. Abandon all hope

I was at my mom's one day and I noticed she had two catalogs sitting on the kitchen counter. One was for a company that sold nothing but muumuus and housecoats that zip up the front, because when you're old, putting on things over your head is hard. The other consisted of thirty full-color pages of wigs. I'd never seen my mother wear a housecoat or a wig, so I was quite surprised to see these catalogs in plain view, pages dog-eared. *Did my mom subscribe to these?* I wondered. *Or do you just reach a certain age and they send them to you?*

Before I realized what I was doing, I found myself flipping through the catalogs and imagining what I'd look like in a Mrs. Roper–inspired muumuu and a Jaclyn Smith–edition bob. And, to be honest, I wasn't hating what I envisioned.

In my opinion, a caftan is always a good solid style choice.

It's comfy because it's half-dress half-robe. It hugs the curves, but it doesn't grip them and show every ripple and dimple. And it would make figuring out what to wear every day a lot easier if I could just zip myself into a grandma gown. I wouldn't need undergarments and I'd get a nice breeze in the summertime to air out my occasional swamp crotch. According to the catalog, if you invest wisely, a good house dress can go from coffee on the porch to lunch with friends to a wedding in the evening with just a change of accessories!

And let's talk about wigs for a minute. Wouldn't it be nice to have The Rachel one day and clip-on bangs the next? How many of us have ruined a good eight to ten months of our lives by cutting bangs when we should not have? Also I could finally stop spending so much money dyeing my hair. I could even shave my head and save on shampoo!

While this path sounded good, in the end I decided to at least wait another fifteen years or so before I embraced it.

3. Age gracefully with some mind-over-body stuff

Spoiler alert: This is the path I chose, as it makes the most sense to me. I've continued dyeing my hair and waxing my lip, and maybe one day I'll add a few minor cosmetic procedures. When I get tired of frowning, I'll consider getting a little Botox here and there. I may get my disappearing eyebrows microbladed and add to my fading lash line. It wasn't hard to up my moisturizing regimen from once a day to twice; and I throw in a serum and a mask here and there to fight whatever the "signs of aging" are. Instead of caftans, I embraced "fit and flare" dresses and upped my budget for expensive shapewear and cute but sensible shoes.

I'm not there quite yet, but eventually I'll start hanging out at Chico's, bopping to the Cranberries on the overhead speakers, and buying their clothes, which are really just Garanimals for the older set. I'll wear statement necklaces and get that "Mom" haircut that's waterfall in the front, blades in the back, because long hair is sweaty when you're hot-flashing. And once my kids are older I'll trade in my minivan for something more fun—judging by the parking lot at Costco, I think the Jeep Wrangler is the female midlife crisis equivalent of the sports car.

I could do all these things, but they wouldn't matter until I fully accepted what was happening to my body and was cool with it. It was the healthiest path, but acceptance was the hardest part. I had to truly believe in it. My mindset was what needed to change. I needed to get my brain on board. I could do all the workouts, ointments, and surgeries I wanted, but if I continued to allow myself to feel old, then I was old. I had to pick my battles and remind myself that aging isn't so bad.

A few months ago I saw my aunt Lorna. "Hey, Jen, look what I found when I was cleaning out my closets!" She waved a glossy eight-by-ten photograph in my face. I immediately recognized it as a twenty-five-year-old souvenir photo from a trip we took together to Portugal. We'd signed up for an "authentic Portuguese dinner" and the photo was included.

I took the picture from her and studied it closely. It was taken the summer after I graduated from college and I'd spent the previous several weeks traveling around Europe before meeting my aunt in Lisbon. I was tanner and thinner than I am now. My face was unblemished, and my hair was frizzy but showed no sign of the gray that was to come. I was a little envious of the youthful girl in the photo until my mom peered over my shoulder and announced, "You look better now. A lot better."

At first I was offended, but then I understood what she meant. In many ways I looked better at forty-seven than I did at twenty. Sure, some of that had to do with the fact that I now had more money and better taste. When I was twenty I didn't know about the miracle product that is a flatiron, and I thought cargo pants were awesome because I could carry all my shit without the hassle of a purse. But I also didn't possess the confidence that I do now. I didn't know who I was yet. Yes, the girl in the photo was young and carefree. She'd gone off to Europe alone to find herself, like the heroine of one of the novels she devoured, but she was also insecure and unhappy. She didn't like herself. She was at her thinnest but still thought she was fat. She hated being the funny sidekick—she wanted to be the main character in her own story. She didn't know how to talk to people or how to fit in with her peers. And, most important, she had not figured out her purpose yet, so she was angry.

Seeing that photo made me think of my daughter, Adolpha, and the message I was sending her. She was thirteen and watching me for clues as to how to navigate all the bullshit beauty standards and anti-aging messages out there. If nothing else, I needed to embrace a positive attitude for her so that in thirty years she would have an easier time.

I talked to her and told her that yes, I was getting older, and some days it sucked, but most days it was really okay. Because I was aging, but I was also becoming wiser and more confident, and reaching middle age has helped me recognize my priorities. I even told her one of the most controversial opinions among women: *I like myself*. It took me forty-plus years to reach that milestone, but once I did, it was like a weight was lifted. I wasn't so angry anymore. (Okay, fine, I'm still angry, but I'm angry about different shit, stuff that actually matters.) I wasn't so sad anymore. I wasn't so confused anymore. I wasn't so bored anymore. My eyes were opened and I understood what I needed to do going forward. I cut out a lot of shit from my life, and one of those things was my negative outlook about my appearance as I age.

As hard as I try, I have to be reminded constantly, though. And that's where it's good to have friends who will check you and keep you on the right track. I was talking to a friend the other day about a recent photoshoot I'd done. I told her, "There are some bad photos in the lot, but overall I like them."

She replied, "There are no bad photos of ourselves. There are just photos we like better than others." Of course there are still days I am not thrilled with what's going on with my body, but I've tried to embrace a positive outlook and all that good shit. I'm finally content with who I am and how I look. And there are certainly parts of me, both inside and out, that could be improved upon, because I think we should always be looking for ways to improve ourselves, but the *what* and the *how* are up to me to decide—no one else. We all have different ideas of what needs improving as we age, and we should be allowed to age without external pressures being put on us by society, media, our spouses, or other women. My new mantra: You do you and I'll do me. Because the most important thing is being content with yourself. When you're content, everything else falls into place, creating balance.

As a result, I don't beat myself up so much anymore. I don't worry about the number on the tag in my pants or fret over my thinning lips or my graying hair. I no longer compare myself to my friends or to women I see in magazines and ads. I've embraced who I am, and every day I'm working on loving my-self and being content to allow myself to age as gracefully and as naturally as I want to.

JEN'S GEMS

Fuck everyone's opinion. Age whatever way you want.

Who Are You Calling Crazy?

It's Okay to Be Mad as Hell

As I get older, I've noticed how often women are being called crazy. But are we really crazy, or are we just sick of everyone's shit?

Many, many years ago, when I was twenty-two and working at my first job out of college, most of my co-workers were women who were older than me. We were proofreaders at an engineering firm, and the job required us to work in pairs with a different partner each week. We didn't have cubicles or even assigned desks to work at; instead, every week we rotated to a new temporary office with a new partner. Because of this bizarre arrangement I had the chance to spend a lot of one-on-one time with each of the ladies in my group. Because we worked in such close quarters and had a lot of downtime, there was plenty of chatting. At first it would be polite chitchat about the weather, maybe weekend plans, but after a while, the chit-chat about great recipes the whole family will love would take a turn and get a bit more intimate, and as a result, I learned a lot. Probably too much. In those days I was single and living on my own. I wanted a husband and kids, but after spending days on end listening to the women around me lament about their lazy husbands, bratty kids, domineering mothers-in-law, boring sex lives, and money woes, it made me wonder what the fuck I was wishing for exactly.

A married mother of three confided in me that she was actually *losing* money by working. One Monday morning we were assigned to work together, and when I arrived she was already in the office with a coffee and a doughnut.

"Wow, you're here early!" I said. (Everyone I worked with was early, though, because I was always five minutes late.)

She spoke with a mouthful of doughnut. "It was a very long weekend, so I took my kids to daycare early today."

"Oh, did you have a fun weekend with your kids?" I asked, because in my young, childless mind, weekends with kids were a blast. You got to go to the park or play games or watch Disney movies or take naps together. Kids seemed to me like a source of constant entertainment back then.

She scowled at me. "No. I didn't have a fun weekend. My kids were assholes and my husband golfed all weekend. Did you know that coming to work is actually a break for me?"

"What?" I was horrified. We worked in the damp, window-less basement of a cinder block building. We were steps from the cafeteria, and even though fish sticks weren't on the menu every day, it sure as hell smelled like they were.

"The pay here is crap and I *lose* money every month after paying for my kids' daycare, but I can't stand to be around them. It's worth the price to work here just for my sanity, Jen." We spent our days proofreading engineering specifications and memos for pennies. It was a nightmare job, and I was alarmed to hear that motherhood was worse. That someone would actually choose to come to the cesspool we called an office to escape from her hellspawn blew my young, uncluttered mind.

Another woman speculated that her husband was having an affair and she didn't even seem to care. "He's had to 'work late' every night this week," she confessed.

"Well, maybe his boss made him," I said. "What does he do, again?"

"He's a teacher," she said. "On summer break."

"Right. Yeah, that's a tough one," I said. "He's not even trying to hide the affair."

She shrugged. "You know what? As long as he doesn't throw her in my face—or give me a goddamn STD—I won't divorce him. Neither of us can afford our house on our own, and I love my house. Plus, he's a good dad and the kids would be really sad if we split up. And, on the bright side, at least I don't have to have sex with him," she said. "Someone else can do that job now."

My idea of romance was instantly shattered. I looked around at all my co-workers, who I had always presumed were happy, and wondered how many of their marriages were held together by a cozy three-bedroom ranch in a good school district. And what was this about married couples not having to have sex anymore? In those days I still had the energy and drive for sexy time, so I was panicked to learn that there were plenty of married women who didn't. All of the matriarchs of my family (probably in cahoots to keep my virginity intact) had told me that besides children, sex was the greatest part of marriage! Had I been lied to?

I realized that the women I worked with confided in me during the times we were completely alone. In order to do our work properly and catch errors, we were forced to read out loud to one another, situated in small, private rooms that were essentially soundproof. We'd close the door and read, but when there was a lull in the workload, they'd drop these confessions on me. At the time I had no idea why they unloaded on me, but looking back now, I realize that I provided a safe space for them, much as I do today with my online community.

Many of the women I worked with socialized with one another outside the office. But I was rarely invited to join, because a lot of their get-togethers were "middle-age" kind of events. They had birthday parties for their kids, "couples only" dinner parties, and a book club where they discussed *How Stella Got Her Groove Back* by Terry McMillan instead of Chelsea Handler's *My Horizontal Life: A Collection of One-Night Stands.* We didn't have a lot of online communities back then, and I was the closest thing they had. They knew they could gripe about their kids or husbands to me and it would be like going into a black hole, because I'd never meet any of the people they were complaining about. I also didn't try to solve their problems. I couldn't have helped them if I wanted to, because I didn't have any experience with anything they were dealing with. I was the perfect person to just listen and take it all in. And when they were done vomiting up all their dirty little secrets, I'd watch them straighten their spine and put their happy face back on and say something like "Oh, don't worry, Jen, it will be fine. It's just something I have to get through." And then they'd leave our shared office as if nothing had happened. Even when they divulged their most personal or gut-wrenching emotions to me, these women would always whisper their complaints or speak in hushed tones. They never cried or raised their voices. They were always composed and seemed just resigned to their lives.

Except for Joan.

Joan never whispered, and she never pretended middle-age angst was anything but misery. "You know your boobs will sag, your hips will spread, and hair will sprout from places you didn't know could grow hair," she barked.

We were in the women's bathroom at the office. I was washing my hands and she was plucking a wiry gray hair growing from the top of her ear. I was appalled, because I was certain only crones grew hair on their ears and nose. The incredible part of this story is that I had not asked Joan a question. I had barely acknowledged her. This wisdom bomb she dropped came out of nowhere. And I wasn't even sure she was talking to me. She hadn't taken her eyes off the ear hair she was desperately trying to snag with a pair of tweezers, and when I responded, "Excuse me?" she snapped, "Was I talking to you?" Um, I thought so. We were literally the only people in the room.

Everyone in the office was positive she was crazy.

In fact, we all called her Crazy Joan behind her back. Crazy Joan was the oldest person in our department. She was well into her fifties at that point, and she was completely out of fucks to give.

Earlier that year, for Secretaries' Day, our boss took us to the Olive Garden to celebrate with all-you-can-eat salad and breadsticks. Everyone was excited, since we were usually a brown-bag-lunch kind of crowd, but not Crazy Joan. She declared, "So, let me get this straight. The boss gave us some bullshit speech telling us we are the 'lifeblood' of this company, everything would halt if we didn't come to work tomorrow, making seven bucks an hour—before taxes, mind you—and we should kiss the man's ass because he fills us with unlimited breadsticks once a year? Don't you see, lemmings? They're *literally* making you fat and happy so you won't revolt and tear this place down! Open your eyes! Wake up!"

At twenty-two I was just thrilled we got a long lunch, and did I mention the all-you-can-eat breadsticks? Um, yum! A salary *and* perks? I felt like I was winning at the whole job thing.

The rumor around the office was that Crazy Joan had once been a lady of leisure, with a rich husband and a membership at a golf club. But he had a midlife crisis and left her for his secretary. Because she didn't have any work experience, she was forced to take this shitty job. She was barely holding on to her home that also housed her deadbeat adult children and her very ill mother she was caring for.

Crazy Joan was the one person in the office who never confided in me. The walls were thin and she had a booming voice, so I caught snippets of conversation whenever she was assigned next door to me. When we worked together, she spent her downtime in the bathroom (plucking hairs, I assumed) or outside smoking. We rarely chatted. She didn't deem me worthy to unload her secrets upon. I was okay with that, actually, because I was a little afraid of her. I'd never met a woman who said whatever was on her mind without any fear of repercussions or judgment.

One day after the Olive Garden incident, I worked up the guts to ask Crazy Joan if the rumor about her past life as a rich housewife was true. She scoffed. "Close enough!" She smiled, but it was more of a grimace. Then she said, "Fuck this. I need a cigarette." She got up and left the room where we'd been working and didn't return for over an hour.

I sat there waiting for her to come back, alone with my thoughts. Everyone around me was reading quietly, so there was no one to talk to about what had just taken place. Crazy Joan seemed rattled. I knew I'd triggered something, but I wasn't sure what or how. As I sat there, it dawned on me that Crazy Joan wasn't crazy. The story I'd heard wasn't a rumor. It was true—or at least somewhat true. Joan's idyllic life had been upended and everything changed for her and now she was at her fucking wit's end working a shittastic job where everyone called her "crazy" behind her back.

When she came back, I asked, "You good, Joan?"

She didn't reply. She just nodded and picked up the document and started where we'd left off. But our relationship was different after that. Before that moment, Joan had never taken an interest in me or anything I did, but afterward, it was like she was determined to save me from sharing her fate.

Joan was the one who came into my office one day waving a piece of paper. "Jen!" she yelled. "Someone has to make it out of this place. The rest of us are all fucked, but it can be you!" She slapped the paper on my desk. It was a memo detailing the company's paid MBA program.

Ugh. More school? Fuck that. "I don't want an MBA," I argued, pushing the paper away.

"Don't you see? This is the one thing they'll do for you! You have to take advantage of more than just free breadsticks, you dummy! The stuffed suits upstairs will pay for your MBA. Yes, you'll be tied to them for the five years after, but you'll be an executive, and it's a small price to pay for a master's degree. For free! You could do *anything* with that degree," Joan said, shoving the paper back at me. "Put in your five years and then get out of this shithole better than ever!"

"It sounds like a lot of work," I complained. "I don't know if I have time."

"A lot of work? You don't have time?" Joan rolled her eyes. "Is your life so hectic when you leave here at five on the dot every night that you don't have time to go to school? You don't have kids. You don't have a husband. Do you have time-consuming hobbies I don't know about? Are you training for a marathon or something? Do you even have a cat to take care of? *You have nothing but time! And you're wasting it!*"

I bristled. "I have a life," I said. It was none of her business that I liked to be on my couch, sans bra, takeout dinner in hand, by 5:30 so I could watch all my must-see TV. I didn't need to explain my life to Joan. She did not deserve an explanation of what I did in my downtime.

But this time Joan wasn't alone. As I said before, she was quite loud and her voice carried around the floor. My doorway quickly filled up with other middle-aged women.

"Are you going for the MBA program, Jen?" one asked, wistfully. "I'm too old now."

"I wish I could do it," another chimed in. "But it's a night program. My husband works nights, so I have to be home with the kids. Maybe in a few years . . ."

"Jen, this is your chance. You could do this and then be our boss!" another said. "I hope you'd be a nice boss who wouldn't be mad when I need time off to take my kids to the doctor."

Someone said bitterly, "I bet they wouldn't let her do it. This program isn't for us basement dwellers. It's for the people upstairs."

"Oh, I didn't think of that," I said. "She's probably right. They probably wouldn't even let me in."

"Fuck that," Joan spat. "This flyer was in the cafeteria—where *everyone* eats! The program is for anyone—not just the upstairs people. If you want in, Jen, I'll make sure it happens. I'll protest, I'll stage a sit-in, I'll throw a fit. Whatever it takes. Do you want in, Jen?"

I'd only been out of college for a year and I really liked my free time. I didn't want to jump back into studying again so quickly. I was so young. I had *years* to get my MBA if that's what I decided I wanted. I thought of my comfy couch and my endless supply of free nights. "I dunno," I said, slumping in my chair. "I don't even like business. Why would I want an MBA?"

"A *free* MBA," Joan said, poking me in the shoulder.

"It could open a lot of doors for you, Jen," one of my co-workers said.

"The opportunities you'd have . . ." another proffered.

"Meh," I sighed. "I don't think so. I don't want to work here forever"—in those days five years felt like a fucking lifetime to me—"and I don't want to go back to school again already. I'm really enjoying, like, just being an adult, or whatever."

They all stared at me with a mix of envy, pity, and loathing.

"Goddamn youth is wasted on the young," Joan said, glaring at me. "You're making a big fucking mistake."

Now, at forty-seven years old, I want to find Joan and hug her and say, "Yes! I get it. I'm sorry I was a fucking moron back then. Let's both go back in time and slap me across the face."

I get it now. All of it. Joan wasn't crazy. She was just tired of being responsible for everyone else's shit. She was sandwiched between her kids who were using her like an ATM machine and a bedridden mother who lived in her guest room and whose care required whatever money Joan's kids didn't take. And let's not forget that she basically ran that office and made seven goddamn dollars (before taxes) an hour while our boss drove a Mercedes-Benz and took all the credit while talking down to her (now we call that mansplaining, but back then it was just the way men talked to us and we allowed it). She was right to hope he choked on his free breadsticks.

Joan was feeling her feels, and it made everyone else in the room a little uncomfortable. But fuck that. She had been served a shit sandwich and she was mad as hell and she wasn't going to take it anymore. She was not living the life she'd imagined for herself and she was tired of everyone pretending like everything was fine when in fact the world was burning around them.

When Joan and I worked together, I thought I understood her, but I didn't completely understand Joan until I turned forty-five. It's halfway to ninety, and ninety is old as fuck. So that's kinda tough. Sure, I still had three nonagenarian grandparents, but the odds of my making it that far were slim. I drive too fast, drink too much, and eat way too many carbs. So forty-five felt like the true midlife to me. It was all going to be downhill from there.

Joan was in the throes of midlife and was fed the fuck up. She was tired of women calling her crazy and of being invisible to men. And she was especially exhausted by twenty-two-year-old me who had endless opportunities, free time, and energy but couldn't be bothered to take advantage of any of it because I was too busy chilling out. She knew what it felt like to look back on the past twenty-five years and wonder where the fuck it went. She knew that someday I'd wake up and wonder why the hell I wasted all those years, and she was trying to help me.

As I've gotten older, I've become Crazy Joan, and I'm absolutely fine with it. Someone needs to tell the goddamn truth and call out the bullshit, and my middle-aged friends and I are ready for the job. But don't call us crazy. We're not crazy. When we hit our forties everything snapped into focus for us. We can finally see all of the lies we've been fed, all of the injustice in the world, all of the burdens that we've been carrying by ourselves for years. We're finally demanding our fair share and our spot at the table. But when we find the courage to speak up and voice our concerns and list our demands, someone always has the nerve to call us crazy. We aren't crazy. We're finally conscious. We're finally feeling something, and most of the time what we're feeling is rage.

On any normal day, I am a bundle of many different emotions, but rage is always the one that works its way to the top. I might start out the day apathetic or melancholy, but by the end of the day I'm ready to burn shit to the ground. I am furious with everything and everyone around me, so I fucking dare someone to call me crazy one more time and see how it goes.

I am enraged when I think back to all the shitty jobs I've had and the conditions I worked under and the shit I took. I am livid when I look around the world and see nothing but imbalance. I was infuriated when I stayed up late on election night 2016 and watched the most qualified presidential candidate in my lifetime get beaten by a fucking sideshow clown. To me, that summed up everything I'd experienced in my life. I knew so many intelligent, overqualified women who worked tirelessly to get ahead in their jobs, to balance their family and marriage, only to see some well-connected jackass swoop in and take what was rightfully theirs.

Lots of stuff makes me angry, but I think the hypocrisy that we're met with every single day is what sets me off the most. Earlier this week I watched the Senate confirmation hearings for Judge Amy Coney Barrett. Judge Barrett and I have very little in common, personally or politically, and it would be rare to find myself defending her or anything about her. And yet I found myself sitting there on my couch, outraged on her behalf and growling at all the male senators on my television who spent their allotted time praising her for her motherhood. This is a woman who, politics aside, has accomplished many things besides raising seven children, but when questioning her about her qualifications for a place on the highest court in the land, no one could get past the fact that she possessed a working uterus plus a heart, calendar, and car big enough to accommodate seven kids. They marveled at her ability to balance it all, like she was a magical creature they couldn't possibly understand. At one point, a senator even asked her who did the laundry at her house. Are you fucking kidding me? First of all, you are considering this woman for the United States Supreme Court and you're asking her about her laundry? In all the years I've watched male nominees go through the same process, I've never once seen a senator praise a judge for his strong swimmers or ask him who did the laundry in his house. With all due respect, sir, choke on a dick. And second of all, women who can balance their family and work life aren't magic, they're just doing what needs to be done because no one else will do it! Who does the laundry in the senator's house? Probably his magical wife!

No wonder so many middle-aged women have had it! Some

people might argue that rage isn't good for your health, and to them I would say "Fuck you." People are motivated by different things. Some people are motivated by love, and that's okay, that's just not me. I'll never be the one out at the prayer pole singing "Kumbaya." If that works for you, then by all means proceed. We need people to do that too. But for me, it will always be wrath that pushes me into action.

While I can totally identify with Joan and what she went through, there's a fundamental difference between us. Joan gave in to her rage and basically gave up by the time she hit middle age (although, to be fair, she had a lot more to deal with than I do and a lot less support, so she didn't necessarily give up as much as have the deck stacked against her).

I'm lucky because I don't have a corporate job anymore. I don't have a boss to answer to. I can say whatever the fuck I want. I can amplify the voices and the messages that I think are important and need to be heard. I've been given this ability and this time, and I'm not going to waste them.

Once again, I've found myself in a position where I have opportunity, support, time, and now a whole lot of mother-fucking rage motivating me. I've learned from the mistakes of my twenties. I'm not wasting the last half of my life sitting around pantsless on my couch binge-watching Netflix (at least not every night). I'm older and wiser, and like Joan, I am completely out of fucks to give. Middle age has made me angry as hell and I might as well lean into it and use it. I'm taking all of my experience and all of my fury and channeling them into something productive. I could yell into the void, but instead I'm being very judicious about where I'm spending my energy and money. I'm trying to share and support only ideas or organizations that might actually make a positive change for the future generations of women and minorities in this country. There's a lot of talk about privilege these days, and I know I possess an enormous amount of it, so I'm listening and learning and holding space for people who don't have as much. Normal, ordinary women who would have been called crazy paved the way for me, and now I (along with my friends) will do the same for others. So, if you'll excuse me, I just need to go find some matches so they can all follow the light from the bridges we burn.

JEN'S GEMS

You're not crazy. It's just that middle age gives you all the feels. Don't fight them, embrace them and use those emotions to propel you forward to make changes in your life and the lives of those around you. But go easy on the rage. Rage is okay, but let that fire light your path, never consume it, because then you're fucked.

Are We Going to Get Divorced?

Relationships Take Work

I don't know one married couple who make it into midlife together without wondering at some point, *Is this all there is? Shouldn't I feel more fulfilled in my marriage? Will we end up divorced?* By the time you reach fifteen or twenty years together, so much has changed. The honeymoon is over and no one is on their best behavior anymore, and hasn't been for quite some time. As a couple you've seen some shit. You've been through "better or worse, sickness and health," and everything in between. You've celebrated major highs, you've weathered a fair share of lows, and you've slogged through a fuck ton of boring-ass days together.

We'd been married thirteen years when the Hubs announced he wanted to start his own company. Up until that point he'd really focused his energies on helping me achieve *my* dreams. When "People I Want to Punch in the Throat" went viral, it was his idea to capitalize on that opportunity. We worked together to grow the online platform. He was the one who learned about self-publishing and helped me publish my first book, and when I told him I wanted an agent and a traditional publishing deal, he offered ideas to help make that happen.

But after several years of working behind the scenes, he said, "I am proud of what you've accomplished, but I want my own legacy too. I don't want to be known as the guy who held your purse."

I didn't know what to say. It was shocking to hear he felt that way. He'd never been the macho type and had always seemed perfectly content being the man behind the woman. He never complained when I asked him for help (or to hold my purse) and was always thrilled for my success. I had no idea he was harboring these thoughts.

He told me he had a brilliant idea for a start-up and was prepared to do whatever it took to bring it to life. Something you need to understand about the Hubs is that he does nothing small, so he wasn't just thinking about opening a sandwich shop or something. Nah. He wanted to create a company that would rival Facebook or Amazon. He wanted to be a major player, a game changer. I wasn't sure how I felt about this declaration.

On the one hand, I wanted to support his dreams. He'd never balked at anything I wanted to do, but on the other hand, my dreams were more akin to a sandwich shop than to Google. His big idea and his ambitious plan scared me. We were finally getting ahead. It had taken us years to recover from the setbacks we suffered during the recession. We were finally making good money. I was earning an income from writing and he was building his client list with real estate. We were so close to getting out of debt. Here he was dreaming about launching a start-up while I was thinking maybe we could finally remodel our twenty-year-old kitchen or save for retirement.

But we were a team. In all our years together, we'd weathered storms and taken big risks. We'd always lived close to the edge, and we'd learned to appreciate the thrill of doing things our own way. This wouldn't be any different, I figured. If this was what he wanted to try, I couldn't stand in his way. I couldn't dash his desire to achieve something great. I couldn't hurt his pride or make him think I doubted his abilities. So I agreed we should sink everything we had into his new venture. He promised me it would be profitable within a few months.

Poor naïve Hubs. He really believed that when he said it. One of the Hubs's best and worst traits is he never lies (this is not a man you want to ask about a new hairstyle unless you can handle the cold, hard truth), so I know he thought his company would take off quickly. He knew he was shooting for the moon, but he didn't realize just how far away the moon really was. Within a few months we'd blown through thousands of dollars and we had nothing to show for it.

I wasn't mad, though. I figured shit happens in business. I knew the Hubs didn't squander our money. His other best/worst trait is he's a cheap bastard, so I knew he wasn't burning money on stupid shit. I also knew he wasn't fucking around instead of working to make his start-up go. If I had to pick the one thing I love most about the Hubs, it's his determination. If he puts his mind to something, he will practically kill himself to succeed. He gets shit done. I was confident he'd get his business up and running, but it would just take a few more months (and a lot more money) than we'd originally planned for.

I don't know if you've ever started a corporation before, but let me tell you, it's daunting. Ideas are easy and cheap, but the execution of the idea is hard. And it's even harder to execute the idea when funds are limited. We don't have millionaire friends or family. We don't live next door to venture capitalists or bankers. We didn't win the lottery. We were completely on our own with this thing with only our good friends Visa, Mastercard, and Amex in our corner.

The Hubs worked tirelessly on it and we all paid the price—and I'm not just talking about money. Living with someone who is basically a mad genius can be very stressful. The Hubs is someone who wakes up in the middle of the night to pace around the house, trying to solve nonexistent future problems. He's someone who doesn't just have Plan A and Plan B but also Plans C, D, E, F, and G and would like to dissect them with you ad nauseam.

When he wasn't working on his start-up, the Hubs was lecturing me and the kids about his start-up, or yelling at us about absolutely nothing because he was stressed out because of his start-up. Good times.

We were several months into living like this when I went to visit my friend Ginger. She knew the Hubs well because she was one of the few neighbors I liked, but of course the ones I like always end up moving away. We hadn't seen each other for a few years and we were catching up. She'd been following a bit of the Hubs's journey on social media but was still kind of confused about what he was doing exactly.

"How's it going?" she asked. "Is it profitable?"

I snorted. "No."

She looked surprised. "After all this time? Still no?"

I shrugged. "He says Amazon took ten years to make a profit or something like that. He says Facebook took even longer. He says I need to be patient."

Now it was her turn to snort. "For how much longer?"

"Well, in a few months we'll start year two, so I guess at least eight more years?" I sighed.

"What do you think about all this? Honestly?" she asked, concerned.

I felt tears well up and my voice quivered. "I hate it," I whispered. "But I can't tell him that. It would devastate him."

"He needs to know," she insisted.

"He supported my dream," I argued.

"Yeah, but your dream didn't turn you into an asshole around your family. Your dream was profitable from day one. You've never lost money on a book. You're the only one making money now, right?"

I nodded. It was true. Once the Hubs started his business he slowly pulled away from selling real estate and within a few months he was barely selling anything. Our dual-income household was down to one income and it was all on me once again. The pressure was insane and I was trying not to let it get to me, but my mental and physical health were suffering and I was feeling a great deal of anger toward him. "I'm beginning to resent him," I confessed.

Ginger nodded. "That makes sense."

"But that's marriage sometimes, right?" I asked. "You take turns resenting each other."

Ginger shook her head. "I've never resented Lou. And I don't think he's ever resented me. Resentment is bad. It's not normal in a healthy marriage, Jen."

I sighed, because clearly my marriage wasn't healthy! "His temper is so short. He's always mad at the kids. Especially Gomer." I started to cry. "They were always so close, and now I feel like he's ruined their relationship."

"It can't be that bad," Ginger said, sympathetically.

"All he does is yell at him. He yells at all of us, but Gomer more than anyone. He calls him lazy. He's thirteen fucking years old. Of course he's lazy!"

"That's awful," Ginger said.

"I'm tired of the self-pity, too. He's always a victim." I told Ginger about the week before, when I'd bought Gomer new sneakers to replace the pair he'd outgrown. I took him shopping, knowing I'd be dropping some serious cash on a pair of fancy kicks. Thirteen-year-old boys don't want lame sneakers, they want cool sneakers. But Gomer knew money was tight and he was willing to look at the clearance rack with me. He actually found a pair that caught his eye. To me, they looked too bright and too clunky to be cool, but what did I know? I'm a mom who wears orthotic Vans. All I knew was the price wasn't as bad as I'd expected, and if he wanted them, I wasn't about to talk him out of it.

He wore his new shoes home and immediately rushed into the house to show the Hubs. In the past, sneakers had been something they'd had in common. They could talk for hours about the pros and cons of certain brands or styles of sneakers, and Gomer was excited to show off his new shoes. As always, the Hubs was on his laptop. Probably checking his email or updating his Instagram or who knows what the fuck when Gomer ran over to him.

Remember I said Gomer's new sneakers were clunky? Well, they were, and they were a size too big because I wanted to make sure this pair would last him a bit longer than the last pair. He was like a baby giraffe still getting used to his weird long legs. He misjudged where his giant clown shoes were going to land and he stomped right on the Hubs's bare foot.

The Hubs howled in pain and immediately lashed out at Gomer. He called him names and implied that Gomer had intentionally hurt him. I was livid. It was the final straw. I've always tried to be a united front with the Hubs and to take his side in dealing with the kids, but in that moment I was seething and my mama bear reared her head. I had watched the whole thing happen in slow motion. I knew as soon as Gomer took that last step that he was going to land on the Hubs's foot. I'd tried to warn them but I was too late. I saw the look of anguish and horror on Gomer's face when he realized he'd hurt his dad, and I could see it was an accident. I was furious that the Hubs would even think that his own child would do such a thing on purpose.

"This whole thing is bullshit. I can't believe he's acting this way. Honestly, he's being selfish, Jen," Ginger said.

Selfish. The word was like a slap. I'd never thought of the Hubs as selfish. He's always been the most generous member of our family. Whatever you want or need, the Hubs will give it to you. When I'm cold, he gives me all the covers. When I'm hungry, he gives me the last bite of his food. When I'm down, he raises me back up. But I sat there and I let the word wash over me.

Was he being selfish? His company *was* putting a lot in jeopardy for our family. Our finances, his relationship with our kids, our marriage. All because of this stupid start-up. And for what? I felt like all of this heartache was because of his ego. What was so wrong with holding my purse anyway? What was so wrong with supporting me? Was being a househusband and making sure I could be the best provider for our family such an awful role for him? Women were expected to do that shit all the time! Why couldn't he? I'd be a much better provider if he'd actually do the work around the house that a stay-at-home wife would do. Imagine how much work I could get done if he kept the house clean, did the laundry, made meals, managed the calendar, ran the kids everywhere. Not half-assing it like he was doing, but for real. Like a real stay-at-home spouse. Why was staying home and supporting a husband good enough for a woman but suddenly his "mangina" was feeling snubbed and he needed to prove his masculinity or something? I could feel myself getting angry. I thought of all my friends who were stay-at-home moms, and I couldn't imagine one of them ever telling her husband, "I need a legacy too!"

When I got home from seeing Ginger, our conversation festered. It gnawed and picked at me. I started out sad, then quickly found myself mad. I became more and more resentful of the Hubs and his start-up. All I could see was money and time going out and nothing coming in. He'd quit selling real estate and had quit helping me with my work. I had to hire an assistant because he was no longer available.

His temper was shorter than ever and his nerves were fried. When I pointed out his behavior he said, "I don't know why I'm like this."

It's because you're selfish, I thought.

Finally, it all came to a boil. I don't remember what triggered the fight, but I know I said things I'd never said before, and finally I blurted the word out loud. "You're being *selfish*," I said.

The word was a shock to him. I could see how much it hurt

him, but I didn't care at that point. I was angry and ready to fight. I was tired of holding back and staying quiet. I was tired of walking on eggshells in my own house and shielding my kids from his explosive temper. I was tired of making excuses to them about why he was too busy with his start-up and couldn't find time to spend with them. It was time to say how I really felt.

"What about you?" he spat. "Was it selfish of you to quit selling real estate so you could live your dream to write full time?"

His words were intended to hurt me, but they just pissed me off, because fuck him. I flung my words back in his face. "I worked two full-time jobs for years! I sold real estate until I made as much or more money writing and *then* I quit selling houses! So no, I'm not selfish. If I spent as much time and money on pursuing a career in writing as you have on your start-up without a return on my investment, I would have quit ages ago! I would have realized that I was putting my family through hell and risking too much for my stupid fucking egotistical dream! But you won't quit, and that's what makes you selfish!"

We went round and round, but he couldn't see where I was coming from and I definitely couldn't see where he was coming from. There was no convincing either of us and we were getting very hateful. Finally we agreed to call a truce and I asked him to at least set some deadlines. I've always had deadlines for myself and my business, and I know that without a hard-and-fast goal, I would fritter away a lifetime. He needed to set some expectations for himself, and there needed to be rewards (or consequences) if he met (or missed) his goals.

He was reluctant at first, because he argued that his company was still in early stages and everyone who worked for him worked for free. "I can't push them to do the work when I'm not even paying them yet," he said.

I was tired of the excuses. "I don't care. If they want to be a part of this, then they have to meet their deadlines. Do your job and manage them," I demanded.

Several months later, the first deadline came and went and nothing much changed. So we moved the finish line. Every time I thought we'd have a tangible result, the goal changed. To say I was frustrated was an understatement.

Meanwhile, I was struggling to raise two teenagers and manage my own career, which was hitting a bit of a lull—in part because I was too busy doing everything else that needed to be done to give it the attention it needed. When we reached year three, the Hubs decided his start-up would do better if it were based in New York City instead of Kansas City, and he started spending weeks at a time in New York City.

Even though this would leave me at home alone trying to manage everything, I figured it couldn't be worse. At least it would be quiet and we wouldn't fight. Once he left, the kids were actually fairly helpful and we got into a nice rhythm of it being just the three of us. We didn't have to deal with the Hubs shouting at us to be quiet or lecturing us to stop spending money or whatever else we'd done that day to piss him off. Still, although the kids pitched in and helped me, I was still the one managing the bulk of the work of running the household. All while trying to write another book because we needed the money.

That's when I missed a deadline.

I'd never missed a deadline before. Well, that's not true. I'd had to extend another one earlier that year because of my health. I was having trouble with my vision and I physically couldn't get the book written in time, so I extended the deadline, which I eventually made.

But this time, I couldn't even get the book done late. I was still struggling with my health, plus I didn't have the time or the mental bandwidth to even write the damn thing. I know it might be hard to believe, but even writing silly, funny books with f-bombs like commas takes a lot of work and mental fortitude. I just didn't have it in me. Between my deteriorating physical health, my added responsibilities at home, and my overwhelming anxiety, I couldn't get the book started, let alone finished.

It really sucked when I told my editor I wasn't going to make it. I was planning to self-publish that particular book, so this was a freelance editor who counts on the money her writers pay her, and I flaked on her. My stress ended up stressing her out, too, which sent me into a shame spiral. If I'd had the money, I would have sent it to her, but I didn't have any to spare. In fact, the decision to scrap that book was going to be a disaster for me. I *needed* to publish a new book. It had been too long since the last one and my iron wasn't just cooling, it was downright frozen. I *needed* to get something new out there for my readers, and yet I couldn't form a complete sentence, let alone a chapter or a complete book.

This wasn't all the Hubs's fault, but the load he added to my plate didn't help, that's for sure.

The Hubs had been in New York City for a few weeks when I completely lost my shit on a phone call with him. While away, he would call every night to check in and give a debrief of his day. I was trying to brainstorm with him and figure out what we could do for money, but our conversation was stilted and I could tell he wasn't fully engaged. I knew he was on his laptop trying to multitask. I got only about half an hour a day to talk to him and he couldn't put down the fucking computer?

I changed tactics and stopped talking about money. "I'm not happy," I said.

"I know," he replied, absentmindedly. I could hear him click-clacking on his keyboard. "You're never happy."

"No. This isn't my normal thing. Like, I'm not irritated because someone was an asshole at Costco today. *I'm not happy.* With this. With us. With any of this. I'm not happy, and you don't care."

The click-clacking ceased but he stayed silent.

"Do you hear what I'm saying?" I asked.

"Yes," he said.

"You're never here."

"Well, I have to be in New York. We talked about—"

"No. Even when you're here, you're not *here.* You've checked out."

"*I'm* checked out? You're the one having so much fun without me. You love having me gone!"

"Are you fucking kidding me right now? You think it's fun to do all of this by myself? I can't see! I can't work! I have to do everything on my own while you're off finding yourself and creating your fucking legacy and you think I'm having fun? Go fuck yourself." I was sobbing.

He was quiet for a minute and then finally he said quietly, "Are we getting divorced?" I finally had his full attention.

I whispered, "I don't know." Because at that second I really didn't know. I was a mess. I was trapped in a sphere of loneliness, fear, rage, and despair, and divorce sounded like an easy out. And what if we did get divorced? Would my life change a whole lot? I was already alone and shouldering all of the weight—maybe I'd actually feel better if I lost one hundred and fifty pounds of stress-inducing man.

"I'm in this for the long haul," the Hubs said. "You're not getting rid of me that easily." His tone wasn't threatening, but the words felt a bit threatening. They felt constricting and a little controlling.

"You can't just decide that for me," I argued. "What if I want out?"

"We made a vow," the Hubs said. "Till death do us part."

I scoffed. "Are you going to kill me?" I asked.

"Fucking hell, Jen, what's wrong with you? I'm trying to show you how much I love you—how much I'll fight for our relationship—and you're turning me into a psychopath!"

I stifled a giggle. Even when we fight, the Hubs makes me laugh.

"What do you want, Jen?"

What did I want? I wanted things to go back to the way they used to be. Our life together had never been without struggle, but we'd always struggled together. We were no longer a team. We were two different people on very different paths and neither one of us wanted to compromise or budge from our respective path. I wanted me and the kids to be a priority for him again. We felt abandoned by him. He said he was in it for the long haul and yet he'd been thousands of miles away from us for weeks chasing a dream that might never come to fruition. I felt the familiar sensation I recognized from several years ago of being buried alive, but this time it was different. It wasn't just a slump like before. It was bigger, deeper, darker.

And my life was different too. I had a purpose now. I was writing all the time, so my "therapy" should have been working, except writing had become a J-O-B to me and it wasn't just for enjoyment or release anymore. I was fortunate enough to be at a point in my career when I was making money from my writing, but now I had contracts and deadlines and expectations looming over me and I no longer had the time to write anything just for myself. In addition, I had the added pressure of finding even more paying opportunities because the Hubs was no longer selling real estate and I was solely responsible for our bills. I had been working on my relationships and I had a strong network of friends to rely on, so I wasn't alone anymore, but I wasn't leaning on them. I didn't want to be a burden or seen as needy.

"I need help," I said. "I think I'm having a midlife crisis or some stupid shit."

"Maybe you are," he said. "Is it like it was before? When the kids were little?"

"No," I said. "It's worse. It's all the regular shit plus my body is being a fucking asshole. I'm exhausted and everything hurts. I'm on a hormonal roller coaster. I had a fucking hot flash that was so bad I thought about climbing into the deep freeze, for real. I can't do my work because I'm physically and mentally unable. And yes, sometimes I think about divorcing you and that my life would be easier without you. Even though I know that's probably not true."

The Hubs was silent. Finally he asked, "Have you talked to anyone about it?"

"No, who would I tell? My mom would freak the fuck out. My friends would think I'm crazy and say I have nothing to complain about. People would kill for my life and I'm crying like a goddamn lunatic. I'm the only one who feels like this. No one understands what I'm going through."

"Have you tried writing about it?"

"I can't," I said. "I refuse to show my weakness. And it wouldn't matter. Like I said, no one understands. I'm all alone and I'm going crazy."

"You're not weak, Jen. And you're definitely not alone. You should write about all of this."

"Really?" In the past there has never been a topic the Hubs deemed off-limits. He's let me write about anything and everything pertaining to him. Hell, half the time, the worst stuff I wrote was his idea. But I didn't think he could be serious this time. There was no way he would come out looking like anything but the asshole here.

"Really," he sighed. "It's the only way you'll work through it."

When we hung up the phone, it was late, and all I wanted to do was sleep. I had to be up in a few hours to get my kids up and off to school. My calendar was full of doctor appointments for me and extracurricular activities for my kids. I also needed to buy groceries and find special multi-fucking-colored straws for Gomer's science project. The last thing I had time for was to write a self-indulgent blog post about my midlife crisis.

I fell asleep only to wake up a few hours later. My laptop was on the bed beside me. I knew writing would make me feel better, but I was afraid. I was reluctant to share my feelings, because I didn't want to appear weak. I'm always the strong one. I'm always the one who has her shit together. If something needs to be done, you ask Jen. I mean, it's great that everyone thinks I'm so fucking capable, but sometimes it really sucks balls because then I feel like I can never show weakness.

And that's exactly where I was. I was stuck. Because deep down I knew I needed to ask for help, but I was worried what that would mean for me. What was better? Suffer in silence or risk ridicule by admitting my frailty?

I took a deep breath and turned on my laptop and I started typing:

So, I'm pretty sure I'm going through a midlife crisis . . .

That was over a year ago, and I'd like to tell you that the Hubs and I are stronger than ever, but I can't. That would be a lie, and at the beginning of this book I promised not to lie to you. We are still married, and we're working on it every day, but his start-up is still there in the middle of our relationship and it still causes me grief. The difference now is that we talk about it more. I don't let the resentment against him build up. I don't worry about looking weak or even mean. I say whatever is on my mind and he says what's on his. Sometimes it's brutal, but at least we know where we stand. We are still navigating our divergent paths and neither one of us is prepared to give any ground, but we care enough about our relationship to fight—for it and about it. I read somewhere that when couples stop fighting, that's the sign of death for their marriage. We still fight plenty. It's not a healthy way to coexist but it's the only way for us right now.

I'm managing to get through it because now I lean on my community and I've dropped my defenses a bit to let them see the real me. I am open and vulnerable about my shortcomings and I am no longer afraid to ask for help or understanding when I need it. In case you missed the memo, I would like to set the record straight: I'm not as competent as everyone thinks. I do not have my shit together. I get through the day with tons of caffeine, screaming into the void, and rage-crying.

I haven't slept through the night in months thanks to my brain being an asshole. I get my work done only because my fear of failure overrides my urge to go back to bed.

No matter how ideal someone's life might look from the outside, I promise you, no one really has their shit together. We are all muddling through this appalling clusterfuck called midlife as best we can. We all have our struggles, but they're worse when we hide them. Trust is hard, but it's necessary if we are to move through and beyond the pain.

JEN'S GEMS

Make some time every day to check in with your partner and talk. Don't talk about the weather or what's for dinner. That's bullshit. Talk about the hard stuff. Really communicate and trust each other. Always make sure that you're authentic and vulnerable and honest. And while talking is best, duh, fight if you have to, because no relationship gets unstuck in silence.

Let's Talk About Sex, Baby!

Finding Your Pleasure

Sometimes I have to force myself to have sex.

Ugh. Writing that one hurt. It hurt me and it will definitely hurt my husband when he eventually reads this. I promise you, it's not him, it's me. And I mean that one hundred percent. I also promise you, he's well aware of how I feel.

I was never really a sexual creature. I was raised with a fucked-up view of sex. I was a virgin until I was in my twenties because I was told if I slept around I'd be labeled a whore, I would catch a venereal disease, I'd get pregnant, or worse, I'd die of AIDS. I don't remember sex ever being presented to me as something that was good for anything other than procreation. Premarital sex was frowned upon, and the message I received from family, friends, school, and church was that sex was something you did once you were married, but never for pleasure, always for purpose.

And then when you added in a healthy dose of self-loathing, you had a recipe for a frigid girl terrified of sex. I wasn't confident in my body and I didn't like the idea of anyone seeing me naked. I'd read a lot of romance novels and I wasn't a typical heroine. I weighed too much to be thrown into multiple positions and I don't recall a period in my life where my body was ever as toned or taut as the ones described in the novels I devoured. I'd always been a chubby girl with low self-esteem, so it was no surprise that I was awkward around men. (I'd like to go back now and slap that "fat" girl across her face and tell her to go get fucking laid already.)

Before I met the Hubs I spent a lot of my precious time dating fuckwits. Man-boys who had no goals, no ambition, no desire to settle down with anyone. I think nowadays my daughter and her friends would call these guys fuckboys. Every generation has them. They were pretty and I liked to look at them naked, but they were dumb as dirt when they were clothed and had nothing interesting or important to say.

When I was twenty-four, I met the Hubs online. I found him really interesting, but I had no idea what he looked like. I could have been emailing with Jason Momoa for all I knew. As we spent more time chatting virtually, I realized I didn't care as much what he looked like as what he talked about. I liked how his brain worked and I enjoyed his sense of humor (fuckwits never get sarcasm). Lucky me, when we finally met in person, he was pretty cute.

For the first time in my life I found myself with someone I was attracted to physically, intellectually, and emotionally. The whole fucking shebang! That's how I knew the Hubs was the One. Up until that point, it had been either fuckwits or really nice, smart guys who didn't get my juices flowing—literally. Finally, I'd found someone who ticked all the boxes.

The ironic part of this story is that a few weeks into our relationship, I was the one who pushed him to have sex, while the Hubs was the one pumping the brakes. He was like, "I think it's too soon." He wasn't sure he wanted to have sex and I was the Jezebel who whispered sweet nothings in his ear and asked him to consent to taking off his pants.

Now, twenty-odd years later? Not so much. When he stands there naked in front of me, trying to entice me, I'm like, "Put on some clothes, you'll catch a cold!"

Every night when I get undressed for bed I have to warn him, "I'm just putting on my PJs, I'm not down to clown. Like, at all."

Our sex life has become incredibly routine—dare I say boring? I literally put it on my calendar. I do this for two reasons:

Almost always when the Hubs initiates, I'm not in the mood, so I ask for a rain check. I postpone, but I'm like a Lannister and I always pay my debts. So I put the follow-up shag session on my calendar so I can plan for it (and work myself up to the task). I think by now we all understand that men are good to go as soon as they see boobs, but women need a lot of mental shit to happen before they can get their engine running.

"Did I eat a good lunch? But not too much lunch? I'll need energy, but not heartburn."

"Did I shower today? Everything's semifresh, right?"

"Are these undies clean? Screw it, they're coming off anyway."

"Are the kids asleep?"

"Is the door locked?"

"Are the lights low enough that I look good? Or are they so low that I literally can't fucking see?"

"Did I answer the email from Gomer's biology teacher? I better do that before this escalates."

Because we have sex so rarely, the Hubs is always convinced it's been a month since we did. The second reason I keep a calendar is so I can show him and say, "Nope, it was actually Monday because you tried on Saturday and I'd just eaten a big dinner and I was like, 'No, I'll puke' and you were like, 'Yeah, me too. Let's watch Netflix instead' and then I was like, 'I'll put you down for Monday' and so I did and then on Monday I rocked your world. Well, sort of. I mean, like, I did all the work for once."

We rarely try new things, and let me be clear again: This is all *my* fault. The Hubs would literally do anything I asked. When every woman in America got all hot and bothered about *Fifty Shades of Grey*, he was like, "Do you want me to tie you up? Do you want to tie me up? Should we both get tied up? Whatever you want to do, let's do it."

I was like, "Ugh, no thank you, rope burns aren't sexy."

There are a few reasons for this:

1) **I'm not interested in learning new tricks.** A few years ago there was this viral video of a woman named Auntie Angel who taught ladies how to give a blow job with a grapefruit. Basically, you cut a hole in the center of the grapefruit, slide it onto his pecker, blindfold him, and then do your thing as usual except you get an extra dose of vitamin C. The video is amazeballs and I encourage every woman to watch it because Auntie Angel has a real gift.

I watched that video, and once I got over the slurping noises, all I could think was, "What a mess. Who wants to go to all the work to give a blow job and have a sticky grapefruit juice puddle to clean up when you're done?"

Another time I read an article in a men's magazine I found in a doctor's office waiting room that touted twenty positions that weren't missionary. I figured I had a few minutes to kill and maybe I'd surprise the Hubs with my newfound knowledge of "what men really want in the sack." The first move on the list was called the 69 Bridge. The man lies on his back and the woman does a backbend over him and then you just perform the tried-and-true 69 move we all know.

A motherfucking backbend. Fuck. That. Noise.

I find that a lot of the new tricks are really just normal sex shit but with more post-clean-up and more required pregame stretching. Plus, I'm not convinced there's much of an upside for the lady. It seems like a lot of these maneuvers are really designed to enhance the man's pleasure. We all know men are visual creatures, and most of these moves just give him regular old sex but with a better view. Unless there's some sort of hot, magical position where he hits the G-spot *and* I look fifteen pounds lighter and ten years younger, I'm not interested in mixing it up. I have enough to clean, and my back already hurts.

2) **I'm busy.** Tick tock, my to-do list is waiting. Bless the man who can punch out at six o'clock and be like, "I have all night to get down."

First of all, I'd love to see you go "all night," because fifteen minutes seems like an eternity. Second of all, if you have all night to get down, then I have laundry you can fold and bills you can pay.

And it's not just my to-do list. I'm a big reader, and my Kindle is always trying to woo me harder than the Hubs. My Kindle's always like, "Hey, baby, do you know how good I could treat you? I could make you so happy. I *could* actually go all night."

3) **Toys require knowledge.** I like toys, I'll admit it. I have a whole box of whirligigs in my closet and I buy batteries in bulk. I've owned toys for years. Some of my toys are older than my marriage. The Hubs and I have tried the toys, but he's like, "Is there a user's manual or something I can study? I'm not sure what this one does." Or, he gets a little jealous when he does figure out what it does. "Oh shit, Jen, it can do all that at once? How the fuck do I compete with that?" Sometimes it's just easier to take matters into your own hands.

God, I'm a horrible person, aren't I?

I started to wonder if most women in midlife shared a similar lack of interest in sex. I decided to offer an informal, nonscientific study in my online groups, hoping to find some advice to get our freak on again. Instead, I found that hardly anyone was having sex!

On the one hand, it felt great to know I wasn't the only one, but on the other hand, whoa. I was going to have to fix this myself.

I knew the Hubs wasn't thrilled, but he was trying to be patient and understanding with me and I really appreciated that. I understood that a lot of the reason we weren't having enough sex anymore was because of me and my fucked-up-ness, and I needed to get to the bottom of it.

Many, many years ago I was young and struggling to fit in at a new school. A teacher watched me fail horribly and then one day he asked if he could give me some advice. In those days I was suspicious of authority figures, and teachers were the enemy, so I was wary of anything he had to offer. But I was also desperate for a solution, so I said yes.

"You have to love yourself before anyone else can love you," he said. "Work on loving you first."

I was sixteen years old and this sounded like garbage to me. *What sixteen-year-old girl loves herself?* I thought. *Fuck this guy and his stupid advice.*

But almost forty years later, Mr. Hewett's advice came back to me.

Sure, over the years I'd been working on my confidence and finding my voice and attracting great people to me, but I was still talking a lot of trash to myself. I was still treating myself like an afterthought. I was still denying myself happiness and pleasure.

Pleasure!

That's what was missing from our sex life! We could have sex on our heads dangling from an airplane wing, but if I kept denying myself the pleasure of just handing myself over to the whims of passion, sex was never going to be good.

When I was younger, sex was new and exciting and taboo, so I liked doing it. When the Hubs and I got married, it was romantic and loving and purposeful—we wanted babies. But after that, you're supposed to want to have sex because it feels good to fuck! And the rumor is that it's a stress reliever, and I don't know if you noticed, but I'm hella stressed. Sex is also supposed to reinforce our connection. Neither one of us feels particularly connected these days, so I'm hoping that by having sex on a more regular basis, we'll feel a stronger bond.

Yes, I'm rocking the oldest, wrinkliest, tiredest, softest body I've ever rocked, but I'm also supposed to be in the prime of my sexuality. This is the one thing I do remember learning as a young woman: Middle-aged women are supposedly horny! I just needed to get out of my head and into the act. I needed to stop the negative commentary: *I didn't shave, I don't feel so fresh downtown, I'm so pale, I'm so freckly, my legs are jiggling, my butt is jiggling, God, everything is jiggling. Ugh.*

I made a concerted effort to stop that shit, but it had to start before I got naked. I was still putting the Hubs on my calendar, but now he didn't know he was on the calendar. After I made sure everything was ready to go physically, I worked on the mental part. I reminded myself why I loved him, why I wanted to have sex with him, what I wanted him to do to me, what I wanted to do to him. By the time I got him into bed, I was already warmed up and DTF.

The next hurdle was keeping my brain from being an asshole. I reminded myself that the Hubs didn't give a shit about my jiggly thighs or notice that I sound freaky when I moan or that sometimes I'm trying to hold in a fart. Not anymore! I let that shit rip. This is a man who watched me give birth to two babies, a little toot wasn't going to make a difference at this point. I bought lube and new toys he could try out. I leaned in far to whatever I was feeling and tried to think about literally nothing else except the pleasure I was receiving and giving. I didn't worry if I was too loud, too slutty, too dirty, or too whatever. I did what I wanted, and—spoiler alert—we both liked it.

Listen, I'm never going to do a backbend, ever, let alone during sex, but if the Hubs brings home grapefruits one day and asks me if I'm interested in trying something new, I'll say, "Only if you mop the floor when we're done, because that shit might be hot, but it's still messy."

JEN'S GEMS

Put sex on the calendar and don't let anything get in the way of making that magic happen. Sex is all about pleasure, so make it fun rather than a chore. When you're finally getting down and dirty, get out of your head and into your bed (or floor or kitchen table or backseat of the minivan). Let go and enjoy the moment. And if you get into a rut, remember: Stretching and grapefruit can't hurt.

Say Yes More. Unless You Mean No. But Try Yes

Leaving Your Comfort Zone

So a few years back, many of us women began to lean in more. To say yes whenever an opportunity presented itself. Nowadays, I'm noticing a trend that is just the opposite. These days you acquire cool points every time you say no to something.

- No to new friends.
- No to signing up to volunteer at school.
- No to new responsibilities.
- No to sugar.
- No to pants. I like the no pants rule, actually. Pants suck. I'll allow it.

Seriously, though, I get it. We're experiencing a natural backlash to all that leaning in we did a few years ago. Women must say no for self-preservation. Many of us work full time outside the home, and at the end of the day, when we step back inside our home, we have a whole bunch of other jobs to do as well. We're being asked to juggle corporate responsibilities and manage relationships with our spouses and our kids and our parents. We're expected to do a lot of the domestic heavy lifting and we need to take some shit off our plates. The stay-at-home moms don't have it any better, because they have many of the same responsibilities without the ability to escape to an office for a few hours a day.

Saying no has practically become a form of self-care.

The other day I overheard a woman say, "I've been reading a lot of self-help books and I've learned to say no to everything now because I'm worth it."

Really? Is that where we are now?

Okay, hear me out. Of course you should be saying no to Meatloaf Mondays at your mother-in-law's house—let your husband and his mom enjoy some quality one-on-one time together over a hot plate of mystery meat. Not for you. And you should definitely be saying no to chairing the school carnival committee—let some other chump take a turn, you've done your time. And you should maybe even say no to your boss—if you feel really strongly against something you are being asked to do, but let's not get fired! But when you say no all the time, you're missing out on some really great people and experiences.

Trust me. I know, because until recently I was the Queen of No.

Nope, that's not true. I used to be the Queen of Yes. Many years ago, when I was a real estate agent, my mentor told me I should join every club and organization that would welcome me as a member, and I should attend every party I was invited to just so I could network the shit out of those things. His advice was simple: Want to get more clients, Jen? Sponsor a Little League team! Want to sell more houses, Jen? Volunteer to usher at the school musical! Want to close more deals, Jen? Join a private networking group! He counseled me to get myself and my flawless elevator pitch in front of as many ripe new homebuyers or sellers as I could and convince them I was the agent for them. So I said yes to everything. I joined the Homeowners Association Board of Directors, I was president of the PTA, I became a dues-paying member of every networking organization you can think of, I was a semiprofessional volunteer, and I attended every Pampered Chef, Avon, and sex toy party I was invited to. I didn't do those things because I wanted to, I did those things because they were "good for business." My calendar was ridiculously full and I was miserable. Looking back now, I see what he was trying to do. In theory, this is a great way to mix business and pleasure, to find that elusive work-life balance. He was trying to teach me that as a realtor, you have to network, so you might as well network in places you want to be. But I fucked it up. I was supposed to do things that actually interested *me*. Instead I ended up doing what had worked for my mentor—a sixty-year-old dude. He sponsored a Little League team because he loved baseball. He enjoyed spending his free time watching kids that weren't his run the bases at the ball fields. He spent a lot of time working with the high school theater department because he'd been a theater kid growing up. It was where he felt he belonged and he wanted to give back to that particular community. He joined a private networking group because that's what old men do. Every week a chiropractor, a banker, and an accountant would join him for golf so they could swap leads with one another while also getting in their eighteen holes. My kids weren't into sports at that time, I wasn't a theater kid, and I had no idea how to golf. Of course I was overwhelmed!

When I quit selling real estate, I stopped saying yes. I stopped sponsoring teams my kids didn't play on and volunteering for organizations I didn't give a fuck about. I left every networking group without even saying goodbye. And I replied "No, thank you" to every jewelry, makeup, or clothing party (and every cookie exchange) I was invited to. It felt amazing to look at my calendar and see so many openings.

I had chosen to leave real estate so that I could write full time. I still had to sell myself and my writing, but now I could do it without leaving my bed or putting on pants (I told you I hate pants). It was a glorious time for several years. I was alone but not lonely. Because I was on social media every day, I still felt connected to my friends. I would comment on their back-to-school photos about how much their kids had grown since last year, I would heart their beach vacation pictures, and I'd sad-face their posts about the loss of a pet. I had the best of both worlds. I could stay home and not shower and still be part of the world.

But then one day I saw Hannah and Page, two women I'd been close to for years, share a picture on Facebook. It was a picture of themselves celebrating Hannah's birthday. *I missed the invitation to Hannah's birthday party?* I thought. I went through all my emails (even the Spam folder) and my unread text messages, but I couldn't find an invite to the party. I went back to the photo to take another look. They were in Page's kitchen. I recognized the cupboards, but the counters were new. *When did Page get new countertops?* I wondered. I realized I hadn't been in Page's home in close to two years at that point. And neither Page nor Hannah had been in my house during that time either. *Has it really been that long? When did I see them last?* I remembered running into Page at the grocery store a year or so ago. I know it was Super Bowl Sunday because the store was empty and we joked that we were the only two people in town who didn't give a shit about football. We did the whole endless loop chitchat thing where we caught up on kids, husbands, life, and other assorted stuff, and then Page said, "We should get together sometime!"

"Yes!" I agreed. But neither of us pulled out our phone and made a plan. *Why didn't we make a plan?* I thought as I studied the photo closer. That's when I finally noticed the third woman in the picture. The woman and Page bookended Hannah. *Who the fuck is that?* I enlarged the photo to get a better look. I didn't recognize her at all. I know all of Page and Hannah's friends, but I didn't know her. I read the caption above the photo. "Happy Birthday to my BFF, Hannah!! You are the most kind and generous friend and I'm so glad I met you and Page! #threeamigos" It was written by someone named Polly. I assumed she was the third woman in the photo. The one in my spot.

I would like to tell you that I didn't care about this photo. That it meant nothing to me. But that would be a lie. This photo hurt. At first I was pissed at Hannah and Page. I was pissed that they'd have a party and not invite me. I was pissed that they'd let some stranger into our circle to replace me. I was pissed that they used stupid hashtags like three amigos.

But once I calmed down, I realized it wasn't them, it was me. Yes, they hadn't kept in touch with me, but I hadn't kept in touch with them either. I didn't pull out my phone that day in the grocery store and nail down a date with Page. I'd not only pulled away from all the groups and clubs that were meant to boost my real estate business, I'd also pulled away from my friends. I'd started a new job that none of them could understand and I'd given up trying to explain myself to them. I had drinks with Hannah and Page the week my Elf on the Shelf post was going viral on my blog. "I don't get it," Page said.

"One million people read my blog post," I said, grinning foolishly. "Can you believe it?"

"But why would you want a bunch of weirdos on the Internet to read your work? It seems creepy to me." She shrugged.

I was irritated because I wanted her to think what I'd done was cool. I wanted her to be excited for me and to see the opportunity this posed for me. "I've always wanted to be a writer, and this is my chance," I explained. "I need those 'weirdos.' And don't call them that. They're not weirdos."

"Yeah, but you can't make writing a real job," Hannah said. "It's a hobby."

Hannah and Page had always looked at my writing as a pastime or a diversion. As something I did when I should be doing laundry or having sex with my husband. They saw it as a time waster and a frivolous dream. After that exchange I pulled away from most of my friends, because if my two closest friends couldn't be happy for me, what could I expect from others?

I was burnt out on volunteering and heading up every committee I could find and I had a new career path in front of me that was going to take a lot of work. I was happy to kick that shit to the curb, even my friends. Friendship is hard. It takes work and I didn't have the bandwidth for it. I didn't make it a priority. I quit calling my friends and they quit calling me. I worked all the time, so I barely left my house, and when I did

I looked like a homeless person. I barely had time to brush my hair, let alone have lunch with a friend. Not only did I see it as a disruption to my writing, lunch with a friend meant the mental and physical toll of showering, grooming, wearing a bra *and* pants, and making small talk.

But I was wrong. It took me a few years to see it, but I see it now. I was dead wrong. When I stopped saying yes, my life started going to shit. I put on weight (that's what happens when your fat ass sits in a chair all day and never moves). I wasn't taking care of myself and I felt physically and mentally unwell. I found myself going days without talking to anyone except my immediate family and maybe my mom. My online persona didn't change at all. I was still cracking jokes and creating entertaining content for my community, but my real-life persona changed drastically. Suddenly I was the woman who dreaded leaving her house. I couldn't sleep through the night. And I definitely didn't want to cook, clean my house, or have sex with my husband. (Oh wait, I still don't want to do any of those things . . .) I was lonely and a bit depressed. I love my husband and my kids, but sometimes they're not enough. Sometimes you need to recharge your batteries by hanging around new people and trying out new experiences other than weekly trips to the post office and Costco.

I realized at that point that I was going to have to become the Queen of Maybe. And not the maybe you use with your kids when you really mean no but you're saying maybe so they'll shut the fuck up already. I'm talking about keeping an open mind and figuring out what is worth your precious free time. We're all busy. We all have crammed schedules, but we all have some free time we could use to say yes to a new opportunity and make a new friend or find a new passion or just care about ourselves. You have to decide what's worth putting on a bra and pants and leaving your house and braving people.

I hear so many of my peers complaining about their lack of friends or purpose or just fun in their lives. So many women tell me they want to make friends and they want to find a group where they belong or try new things, but at the same time, they're reluctant to leave their homes, venture out after dark, go anywhere alone, ask a friend out, join a club, take up a hobby. And they always hide behind excuses like they don't have time. I call bullshit! Your job isn't that stressful or that time-consuming. You're not brokering world peace or solving the homeless problem. If you *are* working on world peace and/ or homelessness, then I'll give you a pass on lunch, but otherwise you'd better be there. Instead, they say no and sit at home in their jammies and cry into their third glass of wine about how lonely they are.

After I'd written my blog post I started thinking about what was holding me back. Why wasn't I achieving the things I wanted? Why didn't I have friends or happiness in my life? Why was I so hell-bent on staying miserable? I traced a lot of it back to my love of the word "no." It was so easy to say no to everything. Yes, there is power in saying no, and you should definitely use it when you really don't want to do something, like clean the toilet when your husband tells you he missed the bowl, but quit hiding behind it. Stop saying no as a knee-jerk reaction to everything because you're too afraid or too lazy to try something new. Because if you say no too often you're going to miss out on some awesome people and experiences.

I'd been passing on social opportunities and it was time to change that. I made a deal with myself. For the next month I would say yes to everything I could.

I've known Denise Grover Swank casually for years because we're both local authors. Every now and again our paths would cross and we'd end up at a book signing together and we were always very friendly while we talked shop. At the end of our conversations one of us would inevitably say "We should hang out sometime," but we never followed up. We'd both get busy with work and family and forget until the next book signing.

So I was surprised when Denise actually sent me a message out of the blue asking if I wanted to collaborate on a podcast with her. I've been a guest on countless podcasts but I've never hosted one. I didn't know anything about podcasting and neither did Denise, but I liked Denise a lot. I respected her as an author and I enjoyed her as a person. I felt I was being given an opportunity that I should say yes to. Sure, our podcast might suck balls, but we'd learn a lot from our mistakes and I'd make a new friend, so I wouldn't be failing alone! I jumped at the chance and we started recording "Two Midlife Mommas" out of her home office later that week.

On one of the first episodes we recorded, we talked about female friendships and how we both found ourselves alone a lot. I suggested on-air that we go and see a movie together, and Denise accepted. We made a date, and a few weeks later, we found ourselves in the theater. At the end of the movie, we parted ways. I had an hour before I needed to pick up my kids from school and I was going to run to Trader Joe's. I briefly thought of inviting Denise to join me and continue our date winding through the aisles of Trader Joe's, but then I totally overthought it and let my brain convince me that was dumbest idea I've ever had. *Why would she want to go grocery shopping with you?* I thought. *That's so weird. Do. Not. Ask. Her.*

Later that day I was home from my shopping and I made a

joke on social media about my dumb idea of inviting Denise to Trader Joe's (because I'm much braver online than I am in person) and she immediately chimed in with "I would have loved that! Let's do it next time!"

Stupid brain.

I've said it before and I'll say it again: Fear is what is holding us back from so much in our lives. I was afraid Denise would think I was a creeper for inviting her to grocery-shop with me, I was worried she'd judge me for buying six cans of chai at a time (we really like our chai around here), I was afraid she'd laugh at me for thinking a grocery store was a fun place to go.

This past year I've tried to say yes to anything that even remotely interested me. I figured it wouldn't hurt to at least try something once. I said yes to attending a fundraiser where I had to dress up like a flapper. I hate costumes because they draw attention to you and I don't like attention. Kind of. I know, I'm an enigma! I like attention online because of what I say (in fact, I love that kind of attention), but I hate attention in person because I look silly wearing a costume. But I did it. And I rocked that costume. I said yes to a girls' trip to Las Vegas. I've never gone on a trip without the family that wasn't work-related. I went to Vegas and shopped and ate and went to a concert and never worried for a second about what my family was doing at home. (Sorry, family!) I said yes to dozens of coffee dates and lunches. Even the not-so-good ones were great because food was involved. I said yes to game nights and pool parties. I do love a good game night, so those weren't hard to say yes to. But pool parties? Are you fucking kidding me? You have to wear a bathing suit or else you actually draw even more attention to yourself than just shoving your pasty, puffy body into a Lycra suit and throwing a fabulous caftan over it. In the past year I said yes to a socially distanced family vacation in the mountains during the pandemic and I even rode an alpine slide and went whitewater rafting. I said yes to adopting a fucking dog. He literally arrives tomorrow and I won't lie, I'm second-guessing myself on that decision. By the time this book comes out, we all know I'll be a certified hashtag dogmom. I still say no to Meatloaf Mondays with my mother-in-law and to running clubs. I'm not besties with everyone I said yes to, and I didn't love everything I tried, but by saying yes, I made a lot of good friends this year and my life is richer for the experiences I had. I have a podcast (and a dog!) now and I've developed close friendships with people who I like to be around and who I can call the next time I'm stuck on the side of the highway with a broken-down car.

JEN'S GEMS

Try to say yes to everything you can for a month. Except Meatloaf Mondays. Nobody should ever have to say yes to that. But everything else? Yes!

"Want to get coffee?" Yes.

"Let's go for a bike ride." Yes.

"I want to go to the Grand Canyon." Hell yes.

"I signed us up for a triathlon." Are you fucking kidding me? I mean, yes. Damn you, Jen.

I would be shocked if you didn't have just a little bit of fun. I mean, the triathlon might suck, but when you finish you'll be able to put "Triathlete" on your business cards and that is badass.

No One Gives a Shit About You

Stop Worrying About What Everybody Thinks

I don't mean for this to sound harsh, but I need to tell you something important: No one gives a shit about you.

Hang on, before you throw this book across the room and switch over to Netflix, let me explain. I don't mean no one loves you. I'm not talking about your mom or your spouse or your best friend. There will always be people in your life who love you and give a shit about you. No, I'm talking about all of those superficial acquaintances and strangers you worry way too much about. The people who keep you up at night. The ones who make you feel awkward or weird or less than.

Those people don't give a fuck what you do. They could not give less of a shit what you're wearing, how you look, how you parent, what your job is, none of it. And you shouldn't give a fuck about them. So stop giving them space in your head.

Over the years, I've written a lot about people in my town. Nobody is off-limits and my own neighbors make my Punch List a lot. I don't feel bad about it, though. If they wanted to stay off the list, they wouldn't be assholes. Basically, if I see bullshit, I call it out. Many times when I give an interview, I'm asked, "What do your neighbors think about your writing?"

And my response is always the same: "I doubt my neighbors ever think about me or my writing at all."

That answer always gets a laugh, but that's not my intention. I'm not trying to be funny. I'm being one hundred percent honest. I don't flatter myself that my neighbors are spending their precious free time reading what I write and discussing me and my opinions. They're assholes who barely remember my name, so why would I think they care what I have to say? I am insignificant in their world. I am not worth the bother.

It takes women decades to learn this. It's usually not until we hit our forties that we begin to understand what "no fucks given" really means. I'm lucky. I've not given a fuck in years, because for once in my life, I was ahead of the curve. I figured out this lovely midlife secret at a very young age.

I graduated from a small Christian college, and the inside joke was that the sales pitch to our parents was "A ring by spring or your money back." Everyone in my class was engaged or married before we graduated, and when our fifth reunion rolled around I knew all my friends would have a spouse, a couple of kids, probably a house, real jobs, and a savings account. At first I was excited to go. I wanted to see everyone and catch up on their new, exciting adult lives, but as the weekend drew closer, I felt an overwhelming sense of anxiety and doom. Suddenly I wanted to cancel. I dreaded anyone asking me, "What's new, Jen? What are you up to these days?"

I had nothing to talk about. At that time my life was a bit of a shambles, personally and professionally. I was sure everyone else had their shit together while I was failing miserably and still trying to figure out what to do with myself, and I was positive they would judge me harshly.

I was single and childless (I didn't even have a dog to brag about back then). I lived alone with no strings attached and couldn't even boast about how hard I was partying, ask them to check out my new kick-ass tattoo, or enthrall everyone with stories about jetting off to fabulous locales with my cool single friends because in all honesty, my parents were my closest friends. Plus, I couldn't afford to jet off anywhere, since I'd recently been fired from my dreary job for stepping on the wrong toes and getting sideways with the mistress of my boss (try telling that to the Human Resources manager when they call you in to talk about how it's been brought to their attention that you're "not a team player"). I didn't even have a new car to show off—I was still driving the same one I had driven in college. Not to mention I'd never lost my freshman fifteen and I'd probably put on another ten since graduation.

The day before the reunion I shared my fears with my mom, and she told me I was being silly. "I promise you, no one cares," she said. "And if they do, they're not your real friends."

I rolled my eyes because that was of course the ultimate mom response!

That said, I gathered up whatever courage I had and arrived on campus the next day. I found everyone at the football stadium. No one was watching the game, they were all clumped in groups chatting excitedly with one another while their toddlers ate dirt and snotted on everything. I could see women showing off new jewelry ("My push present," one announced proudly) and passing around actual scrapbooks of their children's first years. (Remember carrying little photo albums in your purse before cellphones existed? No wonder our backs hurt so much now, we were actual pack mules back then!) Men were exchanging business cards and golf tips.

This is going to be horrible, I thought as I approached them. *Here goes nothing.*

I immediately imagined spinning my tales of woe into a better light. I was fully prepared to throw out better-sounding corporate buzzwords to make my firing more digestible. "I've been downsized" or "I'm in between jobs right now" sounded better than "The boss's mistress was afraid I would rat her out to her husband after I caught them boning in the ladies' restroom at the office." I thought about saying how unemployment was actually a "blessing in disguise" because now I could look at a lot of different prospects and since I was single I could take advantage of any opportunity. I could do anything I wanted since I wasn't tied down to a husband, kids, and a house payment. I practiced keeping my face humble and neutral while claiming, "I'm even looking at jobs in Europe."

I wasn't lying. I was just avoiding the truth. I had *looked* at job openings in Europe, I just hadn't *applied* for any. And if I ever did get off my ass and apply for a job in Europe, I could totally accept it because there wasn't a husband or kids or even a dog in the picture to stop me. I could probably sell my car to pay for my plane ticket. It was worth at least a coach ticket to France.

I joined the group and steeled myself for the inevitable flurry of nosy questions:

"Why are you still single, Jen?" *(Because I'm picky as hell and I don't need a man to complete me like some people here. Ahem.)*

"If you're in between jobs, how are you paying your bills? Oh my god, did you have to move back home?" *(Of course not! I would never live with my parents again! They're totally covering my rent for me because they don't want to live with me either.)*

"Wow, are you still driving your Jeep? We have a minivan. It's ah-*may*-zing." *(Are you serious right now? Am I supposed to be jealous of a minivan? As if.)*

I anticipated the pitying arm pats and the condescending smiles. I imagined all of my friends making eye contact over my head and sort of shrugging at one another and mouthing "Poor thing" and "Total loser."

But none of that happened.

Not one person asked me what I was doing. They were all so self-centered they could only talk about themselves. The conversation completely revolved around them telling me all the incredible and amazing things they'd done since I'd seen them five years ago. Spoiler alert: It was only incredible and amazing if I allowed myself to be impressed by a bunch of people living lives as ordinary and boring as my own.

No one asked me a single question. Not even if I'd changed my hairstyle. (Which I had, by the way, and it was so much better than the frizzy perm and gravity-defying bangs I had in college, thank you very much!)

I'm not calling my old college friends bad people. This is normal. This is what I'm trying to tell you! See? No one cares about you. They're only worried about themselves. You know that everyone had agonized over and carefully curated what they wanted to say that day. They had fussed and worried about how they'd make their average, normal lives sound exciting. They had painted their careers in the best light and every single one of their children was a goddamn prodigy.

I haven't been back to another class reunion in years, but I bet if I went now, people still wouldn't give a shit about what I'm doing, and I have a lot to brag about this time! I'd roll into town behind the wheel of my badass minivan (because down the road I'd embrace the swagger wagon life) with my loving husband and adorable (nonprodigy) kids in tow. I'd have the best hair I've *ever* had and business cards that let them all know I'm now a *New York Times* bestselling author. Plus, my husband, ever the hype man, would seamlessly work into conversation the fact that I have more than a million fans on social media. And they still wouldn't bat an eye. Because we're assuming anyone would even ask!

We have to let that shit go, ladies. Trust me. No one gives a shit about you!

Hang on, again. Like everything else in this book, there's another side to what I'm saying here.

I lied to you right then. There are a *few* people who give a shit about you.

We all have those assholes in our life who like to secretly keep up with us behind the scenes. Those are *frenemies*. Once you stop giving a shit what others think and you find your confidence and start to like yourself, you'll lose friends. It's inevitable. There will always be one or two people who gossip about your career or your relationships or make a snide comment about your new bangs. They give a shit because *they* are miserable cows. They behave this way because they only feel better when they're around others who don't have any confidence and are unsuccessful. These people thrive on others' insecurities. They don't count, though. Those people can go straight to hell because we don't care what they think!

You're taking up space in their head and that's fine as long as you don't give them any space in yours. When you acknowledge that their opinion matters to you, you're giving them oxygen. You're giving them sunlight and encouraging them to grow. That's not good for you—or them.

And let's just say, hypothetically, you're that person. The one who is spending way too much time poring over all the details of someone else's life, relationships, wardrobe, etc. You need to grow the fuck up and get a grip on yourself. (And find a hobby that doesn't include stalking.)

As much as the world tries to convince us otherwise, women are not each other's enemies. We are not here to judge one another and tear one another down. Middle age fucking sucks and the last thing we need is to be critical of how each of us is managing this particular shit show. Instead, we need to be supporting one another. If you're wasting your time giving a shit about the women around you, you're just making yourself depressed, because nothing good can come from your obsession.

Forget these frenemies, though. They're far and few between. Most people are completely self-absorbed and tend to be hyperfocused on what everyone thinks of *them* rather than the other way around. Can you believe it? Do you understand what I'm saying? How many years have you wasted worrying about what the neighbors or your friends or perfect strangers think of you? How many nights have you lain awake replaying every awkward moment in your life? How many invitations have you declined because you didn't have the strength or the confidence to go because you were so concerned that everyone knew every "horrible" thing about you? We have squandered so many good opportunities because we gave in to that fear! Remember:

No one gives a shit what you look like in a bathing suit.

No one gives a shit what you fed your kids for dinner tonight.

No one gives a shit what car you drive.

No one gives a shit about your job.

No one gives a shit about your wrinkles.

No one gives a shit about your bank account.

A little bit louder for the people in the back: *Oh my god, no one gives a shit about you, so stop fucking worrying about it all the time!*

JEN'S GEMS

Hey! I'm fucking serious here. I don't care what your asshole brain is telling you or what you think you know. I don't mean to be rude, but your brain is a bit of a liar. Whenever I feel like my brain is being an asshole, I ask myself if I'd speak to a friend the way I'm speaking to myself. Of course I wouldn't. Because I'm not an asshole! When I feel myself going off the rails, that little question always gets me back on track. And I gently remind myself, "No one (who matters) gives a shit about you, Jen. Go live your life the way you want to live it."

You Will Pee Your Pants

And Not in a Good Way

I'm going to give it to you straight, ladies.

At some point on this midlife journey, you *will* pee your pants.

I'm not telling you this to make you laugh, although you probably should laugh, because it's better than crying and the idea of peeing your pants probably makes you feel like crying. No, I'm telling you this because I promised to tell you everything. I promised not to sugarcoat anything or lie or fluff or make feeble attempts to cover up the truth. I promised to be the most honest guide you could have because we're in this shit together.

Oh wait. Speaking of shit . . .

You will also shit your pants. You will drink a cup of coffee one day and your tummy will do a little rumbly-grumbly and you'll squeak out a tiny fart, only it won't be a fart. It will be a shart. Yes, you read that correctly.

Basically, what I'm trying to tell you is that your body will betray you.

While a shart may happen on a rare occasion, the more recurring problem is your bladder. You can thank your children for that. Actually, I read somewhere that that's not true anymore. Doctors and researchers changed their minds once they found women who'd never given birth also couldn't jump on a trampoline or do squats without the drips. So now they've decided that wetting yourself is just a regular symptom of menopause because midlife bites. We all get to share in the fun. Well, that's just fucking great, right?

Before I hit my forties, I'd heard rumors and whispers about incontinence. I'd even made a few jokes about my mother's weak bladder, but I was an asshole who thought all that nonsense would somehow bypass me. When I quickly skipped past the rows and rows of various pads and adult diapers at the drugstore, I always thought, "That will never be me."

Ha! I could not have been more wrong.

For our seventeenth anniversary, the Hubs and I went to Las Vegas.

If you know anything about me, you're probably wondering *Why Vegas, Jen?* You probably know the Hubs and I are not high rollers, so gambling isn't our thing. Vegas has a lot of shopping and I like to shop, but I'm more of an outlet mall type shopper. I don't think the Wynn has a Crocs outlet store wedged in between Louis Vuitton and Soul Cycle. There are tons of shows we could go see, but the Hubs isn't cultured enough to do that. He'd never shell out a hundred bucks a seat to watch "a bunch of acrobats jump in and out of pools." And yet we still found ourselves in Las Vegas.

It actually checked off a few boxes. Typically, we don't like to spend money on vacations that don't include our kids. We have guilt leaving them home. The few times we've gone anywhere without them, we spend the whole time saying "Oh, the kids would have loved this." But Las Vegas was different. Kids aren't really welcome in Vegas! In fact, we'd probably be singled out as bad parents if we tried to bring our kids into a casino. And we didn't have a lot of guilt about spending too much money because the Hubs had been invited to speak at a conference, so free airfare and hotel room. Yay!

We ditched our kids with the grandparents and headed for the desert with the intention of spending some serious alone time together. Reconnecting. Falling back in love. Relighting the spark. All that good stuff.

Yeah, we had a lot to pack into those three days.

As soon as we arrived, I began to feel sick. I'd been on a perpetual book tour for the previous two years and all of the traveling was starting to catch up with me. Between the dry, smoke-filled air, the time change, and the fact that I had very few responsibilities in Las Vegas, my body decided to go on strike that week.

When I stepped off the plane, I immediately started sniffling, but that was nothing compared to the first sneeze. I sneezed and immediately felt a sensation I'd only recently become aware of. Suddenly I found myself bent in half, with my legs crossed, and working furiously to hold in a dribble. "Oh my god," I whispered to my bladder. "Are you fucking kidding me right now?"

"What the hell, Jen?" the Hubs asked, worried. "Are you having a stroke or something?"

Still doubled over and clenching everything from the waist down, I looked up at him. He seemed genuinely concerned but I hesitated to tell him the truth. Which shocked the hell out of me. The Hubs and I have a very open relationship. I have friends who after fifteen years of marriage still don't admit to their husband that they shit or have shown him their face without makeup. We're not like that. There is no mystery in our marriage. The Hubs knows all of my dirty secrets. He's seen every stretch mark, every fat roll, every undereye bag, he's smelled my farts, he's seen me projectile-vomit, and even after he watched me drop a deuce on the table while I squeezed a baby out of my misshapen vagina, he still gladly went back in there as soon as we got all the all-clear from the doc! What I'm telling you is that nothing scares this guy, and yet I was mortified to tell him that when I sneezed I peed myself.

We were on a fun trip, just the two of us. We had a hotel room all to ourselves and a king-size bed waiting to be romped in. The romance in our relationship was already waning and we were supposed to be using this weekend to get our groove back and I was sure that telling him I tinkled my pants would positively kill the mood.

"I'll be right back," I whimpered.

I still couldn't stand upright without fear of opening the literal floodgates, so I turned and scuttled like a crab to the nearest ladies' room. Once I was safely locked inside a stall, I assessed the damage. The underpants were shot but I'd managed to hold on long enough so the jeans still had a little life left in them; however, I needed to get supplies fast. I shoved some toilet paper in my pants and emerged from the stall.

Maybe one of the women at the sinks could spare a Poise pad?
I thought. *Women carry those, right? Fuck, apparently I need to
start carrying a super-size tampon and a Poise pad because this
is my life now. Ugh.*

A quick glance told me that a miracle wasn't going to happen. Every woman washing her hands or lamenting over her
fine lines (Poor thing, you think those are wrinkles? Just you
wait!) was under thirty. I tried the machines on the wall. Only
tampons. "Damn it, wrong hole," I muttered. Time was running out. I'd just emptied my bladder, so I might have another
fifteen minutes before it filled again. But even a half-full bladder would be a problem if I sneezed again. One more sneeze
and my jeans would be toast and I had only one more pair left.

Damn it, I thought. *Why did I let the Hubs talk me into only
bringing a carry-on? It's free to check luggage on Southwest, you
asshole!*

I understood why my mother travels with eight suitcases. I
assume two of them are filled with Poise pads, super tampons,
Aleve, ice packs, a heating pad, Band-Aids, and an assortment
of Spanx. One is full of all the creams, concealers, makeup, and
that super-duper magnifying mirror a woman of a certain age
requires to maintain her "natural" look. The remaining five
suitcases are all sensible walking shoes, plus extra underwear
and pants for when you pee or shit yourself.

Earlier that morning, when we left Mom at the house with
the kids she asked, "Do you have everything?" She watched me
roll out with a tiny carry-on knowing full well I didn't have
everything I needed! How could she do that to me?

I found the Hubs outside. "You good?" he asked.

"I need to go to the drugstore," I whispered.

"Okay," he said. "Let's get checked in to the hotel first."

"No. I need the drugstore first," I said. "It's important."

"Jen, what is going on?"

"Please, no more questions," I begged.

We went to the closest CVS and I told him to wait in the car.

"You're acting weird, Jen. I think you should let me help you."

I finally relented and allowed him to accompany me inside.

I pulled out my list. "I need cold medicine, soft tissues, lip balm, and . . ." I looked around hoping I could discreetly grab incontinence pads. *Why is this so hard?* I thought. *This is ridiculous. I've never had a problem buying menstrual pads and tampons. Why is this so much more embarrassing?* I knew why it was so embarrassing. Tampons and pads symbolize to the world that you're a young, fertile woman who bleeds regularly and can birth babies. Tampons say, "My uterus is great. I get shit done." Adult diapers say, "My bladder is an asshole. I'm old as fuck."

"And . . . ," he prodded.

"Um, it's just easier for me to get it myself. You get the cold meds, please."

He went off in search of drugs and I found myself shopping in an aisle I'd never set foot in before. I scanned the different offerings. There was everything from pantyliners to full-on disposable undergarments. I finally got a small assortment of different levels of pads, the fuck I was going straight to plastic granny panties.

We met up at the checkout counter and the Hubs surveyed my basket. "Oh. You're on your period," he said.

I hesitated. I could just let him think I was bleeding. He was used to me bleeding. I'd been bleeding for years around him. For some reason the idea of giant, slimy blood clots in my pants sounded so much better than a little urine.

The older lady at the register said, "Honey, you got the wrong kind. You need different pads if you've got your period."

The Hubs looked perplexed. "Well, then what are those for?"

"Umm . . . yes, I understand," I said, trying to give the cashier the secret signal that middle-aged women must give. I figured when I was thirteen and buying my first packages of pads with wings, the women at the registers always gave me a knowing wink and bagged up my purchase quickly, trying to draw as little attention as possible. I assumed middle-aged women had a similar code for incontinence pads.

I was wrong.

The lady said to the Hubs, "Those are for incontinence, not periods."

I strangled a cry and resisted punching her in the throat.

The Hubs is a little daft, so he still didn't get it. "Incont—what?"

She looked at the assortment of tissues and cold medicine I was purchasing and nodded sympathetically. "Oh, honey! Poor thing. You're peezing."

Holy fucking shit!

"You're what?" the Hubs asked.

"Shh, we'll talk about it later," I said, throwing a glance over my shoulder. A line had formed behind us and I was positive everyone in the drugstore was staring at me and my decrepit bladder.

"Jen, what is going on? I'm worried," the Hubs said.

"Oh my god!" I practically yelled. "Okay. Fine! I'm peezing! In the past I've tried to ignore it. But I can't ignore it any longer! Every time I sneeze—or cough, or jump up and down, or squat, or wait too long to find a bathroom—I pee my pants a little! When I sneezed at the airport, I peed my pants and I only brought two pairs of pants with me. I've already lost this pair and I can't afford to lose another! I need the fucking pads to pee on! Just buy the shit. I'll meet you in the car!"

I stormed out, but I could practically hear the whispers: "She peed herself. Do you see a wet spot on her pants? Can you smell it? Ew."

A few minutes later the Hubs joined me in the car with my bag of goodies. "Why didn't you tell me?" he asked. He was half sad and half mad.

"Because it's embarrassing!" I cried. "I am losing control over my body. Everything fucking sucks!"

"Well, at least you don't shit yourself, right?" he said, trying to lighten the mood.

I stared at him. *Fuck it,* I thought, *why am I sheltering him?* I decided to let it all hang out. "Here's the thing. Yes, I pee my pants sometimes. I haven't shit myself—yet. But I have come close. So. Close. I know the day is coming. I live in constant fear every time I fart. My eyesight blows. I can't drive at night because I think everyone has their brights on and I've pumped up the font size on my Kindle and my laptop to where a normal person can read the screen from the other side of the room. The hair on my head is thinning, but the hair on my lip and my chin is thickening and I even found a hair on my nipple last month. My chin hairs are white and I can hardly see them well enough to pluck anymore, so I keep tweezers in the car because that's the best light for pulling hairs! And it's not just my chin! All of my hair is turning gray. *All* of it. I found gray hairs in my eyebrows and my pubes. I don't know if you've noticed, but my vagina is a wasteland. It's dusty and dry and I'm barely interested in having sex. I'd rather read a book than have sex with anyone—not just you. My breasts are lopsided.

One is literally longer than the other. I'm hot and cold all at the same time. I wake up at night in a pool of sweat so I strip down but ten minutes later I'm shivering. I rarely sleep through the night because of the constant peeing, the hot flashes, and oh yeah, my worsening anxiety. I worry about *everything*. Including that I worry too much. I cry about once a week because I'm just fucking overwhelmed by a goddamn roller coaster of emotions. It's better than punching someone in the throat, though, right?"

"Wow, that's . . . a lot, Jen," the Hubs said, frowning. "Is there anything else?"

"Yes. I can't stand listening to you chew your food or slurp soup. You snore so loudly I want to smother you in your sleep some nights but I don't because I love you. And also because I don't have enough gumption to follow through with any of my plans, including murder, because apathy is another real thing I'm dealing with right now. And one more thing: I'm starving."

The Hubs perked up. He's a problem solver, not a listener, and in his opinion, food solves all problems. Especially an all-you-can-stand Las Vegas buffet. "Yes! Let's find some lunch."

A while later I was tucking into my dessert course when the Hubs looked up from his plate. "Do you feel better?" he asked.

I shrugged. On the one hand, I was eating a brownie, but on the other hand, I had a pad the size of a paperback book shoved in the crotch of my jeans.

"Listen, you're doing it again."

"Doing what?" I asked.

"Shutting me out. We're a team, remember? I don't care how weird or embarrassed you feel, you have to let me in. Let me help you. Let me support you. I love you, and I'm in this for the long haul."

I smiled. "Even if I shit my pants?"

"As long as you stay with me when I shit mine," he said.

That, my friends, is true love right there.

JEN'S GEMS

No matter how many precautions you take, you will pee your pants. Always carry two Poise pads so you can help a middle-aged sister out. If you can take only one piece of advice from this book, make it this: Car tweezers are an absolute must. And, for the love of God, always overpack.

Just Be Happy, Damn It!

Finding Your Gratitude

I don't really remember ever being happy. It's not like I'm depressed or anything where I need actual medical attention. It's more like my whole life I've been very "meh," waiting for some sort of magical happiness to descend upon me.

Looking back, maybe I was happy at some point as a little kid. I don't really recall. I know for sure by elementary school I wasn't happy and it just got worse as I progressed through junior high and high school. In those days, I was positive my unhappiness stemmed from a lack of what I'll call *stuff*. If I could just afford the right jeans or sneakers I'd be happy. If I could lose ten pounds I'd be happy. If I could hang out with the right crowd I'd be happy. If I could get better grades I'd be happy.

I bought the jeans (in two different sizes because I lost the weight only to regain it—and more), I made some friends, and I found a subject I could ace. But I still didn't feel happy. I left for college with a new plan for happiness: If I could find a husband and have a couple kids, then I'd be happy. If I could pick a good major and land a great job I'd be happy. *If, if, if* dictated everything in my life. I kept assuming that happiness would come to me in the future. Once I checked off all the right boxes and got everything lined up perfectly, *then* I'd find happiness.

The problem was that a lot of the boxes had in fact been checked, and almost thirty years later, I have so much of the stuff that should make me happy. I have a husband who loves me and supports everything I do. I have good kids. A large, caring extended family. A job I adore. A comfortable home (with a big closet that holds several pairs of the right jeans and sneakers). Most important, we're safe and we're healthy. I'm living a fucking dream life. How could anyone in my position *not* be happy? I'd have to be an asshole to say I'm unhappy, right? And I'm many things, but I try really hard to not be an asshole. And yet I've been living in a perpetual state of general malaise.

Why? Why am I like this? The more I agonized over it, the more I felt—wait for it—*unhappy*. Ugh. Before I knew it I was caught up in a shame spiral where all I could do was go round and round with myself about how stupidly I was behaving. All I could think was, *If you haven't figured out how to achieve happiness in forty-seven years, I can't help you. It should not be this complicated.*

I needed help, but I didn't know where to turn. Yes, I could have picked up any one of the countless self-help books out there about happiness, but to be honest, I really wanted to hear it from someone I trusted. I wanted a friend to look me in the eye and tell me all the secrets to her happiness. I needed my happiest friend to spill the beans.

I didn't want to just lead with "Hey, girl, are you fucking happy or what?" I had to be smoother than that. So I started putting out little feelers. I picked my three closest friends.

I asked Jessica, "When did you feel the happiest in your life?"

After a really long (probably too long) pause, Jessica finally said, "I was happiest when I was pregnant with Aston."

Yikes. Not quite the answer I was looking for. My kiddie mill was closed for business. I didn't care how happy pregnancy might make me, I wasn't going to do that again!

I marked Jessica off my list.

I asked Gabrielle, "What did you do this week that made you happy?"

Gabrielle responded quickly, "I bought new shoes. New shoes always make me happy."

Hmm . . . that felt like more *stuff*, so I marked Gabrielle off my list. And made a mental note to order some shoes. I figured it couldn't hurt!

Finally, I decided to cut to the chase and I asked Matilda, "Are you happy?"

Matilda laughed loudly. "Fuck no," she said. "Are *you*?"

I shook my head. "No, not really."

Matilda was still chuckling when she said, "Yeah, happiness is an illusion created by marketers. They just want to you buy shit to fill the deep, dark, empty hole we all have in our souls."

"Wow. And I thought *I* was dark!" I joked. "But I see what you mean. Like when Gabrielle bought shoes this week."

Matilda frowned. "Maybe. I'm saying, no one is truly happy,

and no matter what you're taught to believe, nothing will make you happy."

"But Jessica said being pregnant with Aston made her happy," I argued.

"Aston's fifteen years old! Think about it! That means Jessica hasn't been happy in fifteen years, Jen!"

I wasn't really surprised that Jessica, Gabrielle, and Matilda couldn't help me. There was a reason we were all such good friends, and it wasn't our rosy outlook on life. No, the glue that held us together was our shared contempt for bullshit and general irritation at everything that we deemed phony. Including, but not limited to, toxic positivity.

A few days later I received an invitation to dinner from my friend Isabel.

We'd barely been served our drinks before Isabel asked me, "Are you happy, Jen?"

I shifted uncomfortably in my seat and took a deep swig from the large margarita in front of me. How the fuck did she know to ask me this question? I wanted to reply, "Of course I'm not happy," but I didn't really want to get that deep with my friend in the middle of my favorite Mexican restaurant. Plus, "friend" might be too strong a word for Isabel. We were more like close acquaintances who meet once in a while for dinners at which we order way too many drinks and complain about our lives. We'd been doing it since we'd met years ago in a moms' group, but ours had always been a very superficial relationship. Hell, I didn't even know her husband's name! We bitched a bit about work/husbands/kids/aging, relayed hilarious memes we'd seen that week on social media, and got a nice buzz going before heading our separate ways for another several months. Isabel was always very nice to me, but I never felt I "knew" her or what she was thinking. We had never jumped into the deep end of the feelings pool and paddled around together. We'd never divulged our secrets or insecurities to each other. Our friendship was not that intense, and in some ways I preferred it that way, because I am uncomfortable with deep conversations in which I am expected to give advice or offer empathy. I am terrible at that, it's completely out of my comfort zone. I'm so much better at rage. I would rather pound my fist on the table and exclaim "What a dick!" than try to give sound, helpful suggestions to anyone's problems. To be honest, I was a bit irritated that Isabel had even asked me. I had joined her for what I thought would be a night of misery loving company, not touchy-feely shit.

I tried to redirect her question. When I am in an awkward situation, I like to make it even more awkward by trying to make people laugh. "I don't know, but if this can't make me happy, nothing will," I said, nudging the huge bowl of chips and queso dip. "Cheese solves all problems and makes everyone happy."

She smiled, but just barely.

Uh-oh, I thought. *This is serious talk if cheesy bad jokes aren't working.* I shuddered. I was going to have to do it. I was going to have to dive in and try to answer her truthfully. What was I so worried about? I'd been trying to figure out the secrets to happiness, and maybe Isabel had them.

"Talk to me," Isabel said. "What's going on, Jen?"

I exhaled deeply. "No. I am not happy. I'm not happy, and I don't know why, and I don't know how to fix it," I said, sadly. I wasn't whining or complaining. I was simply stating a fact.

Isabel nodded.

"Are *you* happy?" I asked her.

Isabel smiled. "I'm working on it. Of course, I don't wake up every morning to birds chirping or anything, but I do try to be happy."

"You *try* to be happy?" I asked, shoving chips into my mouth because eating chips makes me happier than not eating chips.

"Happiness is a choice," Isabel replied. "And every day I choose to be happy."

"That's bullshit," I said. "That's like saying people who have really shitty lives just need to decide to be happy and then your shitty life will be all good. It's easy for you to say you can choose happiness. Your life rocks."

"You think my life rocks?" Isabel said, peering at me.

"Yeah. Your husband—what's his name—he's hot. Your kids are adorable. Your job is kick-ass and you make a shit ton of money. You're gorgeous. You literally have nothing to be unhappy about," I said.

Isabel pursed her lips and then proceeded to unload a shitload of reality on me. "My hot husband is never around. I think I'm a terrible mother and I'm probably screwing up my kids. My kick-ass job sucks the life out of me. It's not what I want to do at all, but I stay because the money is good and I can't justify leaving when they pay me so well. You think I'm gorgeous, but I certainly don't. My whole life I was told I was ugly by the people who supposedly loved me the most. I'm so messed up now I can't leave my house without my armor: a full face of makeup, blown-out hair, and a perfect outfit. My self-esteem is tied completely to my looks, so as I age, it's harder and harder to be confident. And my workouts are borderline obsessive so I won't touch that cheese because it's not even worth how long I'd have to ride my Peloton to burn that junk off my ass."

I was stunned. That was a lot to take in. Who knew Isabel was holding so much inside? "Fuck me, Isabel. I had no idea," I said.

"That's because I choose happiness, Jen," Isabel said. "You are what you choose."

"Okay, but what if you're sick or you've lost someone?"

"Well, that's different, obviously. That's depression or grief. I'm just talking about feeling unfulfilled, untethered. That sort of thing."

"I don't know," I argued. "You can't just put your head in the clouds and be like, 'I choose happiness, motherfuckers!'"

Isabel chuckled. "I think that's the perfect mantra for you."

"So, you just say 'I'm happy' no matter what comes your way?" I asked, pulling the queso closer to me since I no longer needed to pretend I was open to sharing it.

"Yes. I try very hard not to let negativity into my life."

"But negativity is like oxygen for me," I joked.

Isabel didn't laugh. "Yes, and have you ever considered maybe that's why you're not happy, Jen? You are what you attract."

Later that night, I couldn't sleep because I was thinking about my conversation with Isabel. For as long as I'd known her she had been a glass-half-full kind of person. She really did try to see the positive in everything. If I'm being honest, I have to say sometimes it was kind of annoying. Just once I wanted to see her lose her shit and be irritated like the rest of us. But how was it possible she could be so happy when she had so much going on in her head? Compared to Isabel, Jessica, Gabrielle, Matilda, and I had nothing to complain about. We were all dealing with some crap, but nothing like Isabel's, and yet she was the one who was finding happiness and we were all sad sacks. I felt like an even bigger asshole.

For the next few days I tried to will myself to be happy. I'd wake up in the morning and instead of groaning about how noisy the damn birds were, I tried to be positive. I created a Pinterest board with nothing but inspo-porn to help reverse my shitty attitude.

"You will be exactly as happy as you decide to be!"

"Happiness is an inside job!"

"Just be happy!"

After a week of this bullshit, I wanted to murder someone. I was ready to quit when my Pinterest feed showed me a quote that actually forced me to think:

"Happiness is not about getting all you want. It's about appreciating all you have."

Well, shit. Now I felt like an even bigger asshole! Never once had I considered gratitude in the happiness equation, but it made a lot of sense. After that nudge from the universe, I started waking up every morning irritated with the birds, but also grateful that I'd made it through another night and I could hear them and even though the world was kind of fucked up, it was still here and birds were still singing and my kids were safely upstairs and my husband was snoring beside me and I had a job to go to and I had breakfast to eat and all that shit that we take for granted.

Once I added gratitude to the mix, I started to feel a little bit happier.

After a few weeks, I called Isabel. When she answered, I said, "You have to be fucking grateful."

Isabel giggled. "Well, hello to you, too, Jen. What are we talking about?"

"I was looking for the secret and you said I have to choose to be happy."

"Yes."

"But it's more than that. You also have to be grateful for the shit you have. You didn't tell me that part," I said.

"I just assumed most people were grateful," Isabel said.

"Of course I'm fucking grateful," I said. "I just don't always say it. I need to say it more."

Isabel was laughing. " 'Just be happy and fucking grateful.' A self-help book by Jen Mann."

Yes, I believe happiness is a choice, but I also think it's more. There has to be gratitude too. At least for me. In order to be happier, I needed to work on being more grateful. I was taking everything for granted so nothing was making me happy because I just expected it.

I felt ridiculous because I wasn't embracing my positive outlook. I had to let go of my insecurities and just fucking do it.

For years I've been setting boundaries with people who

don't like me, who don't get me, who don't support me, who don't bring me motherfucking joy. For years I have not let them have any space in my physical world or in my head. I'd cut almost all of them out only to figure out that there was still one asshole left. It was me. I was one of my biggest enemies. I was sabotaging my own happiness with anger, resentment, fear, and ingratitude. I was blaming everything and everyone around me instead of looking inside myself and seeing that I was the problem.

I get to decide how I feel about myself and the people around me. The day doesn't run me, I run the day. I set my own schedule and make my own deadlines, so I decide what gets done and what doesn't get done. I decide what sort of day it's going to be. Is it going to be a productive day? Am I going to take charge and get shit done, or am I going to mess around all day and accomplish nothing and feel bad? Or am I going to piss away the day and accomplish nothing because I deserve a day off? Am I going to be content today or am I going to be angry all day? Am I going to worry about things I can't control, or am I going to make the best of the situations I find myself in? Am I going to remember to be fucking grateful?

Now when I wake up every morning I say my little thank-yous to birds, breathing, a roof over my head, family, all that good shit. And then I remind myself that I'm in charge of the day and my happiness is completely up to me. I'm working on it, but I can't help it that sometimes buying shoes and fighting with assholes in my comments section also make me happy. I'm still a little ball of rage a lot of the time, but I'm grateful for the new shoes and the assholes too!

———

JEN'S GEMS

You're the boss of you, and you get to decide if your day is going to suck or not. It sounds kind of stupid, but it's true: Choose happiness. As often as you can. And never forget to be fucking grateful, because without gratitude, you'll never find happiness.

How Are You? For Real

Talking About the Stuff That Matters

I stopped attending parties a few years ago because I couldn't handle the grating small talk. But a few months after I wrote my midlife blog post, I was invited to a networking event that was billed as a women's empowerment night. We were supposed to bring business cards and be prepared to think about how we could help boost one another's career. Normally that's not my kind of thing. But my friend Carla was the mastermind behind the event, and she has dedicated her whole career to bolstering the women around her, including me. I wanted the event to be a huge success and I wanted to support her in any way I could, so I put on my nicest pants (and my best filter) and showed up, because I'm trying to say yes to new opportunities and be a better friend, and I heard that's what friends are supposed to do. Look at me growing and shit!

The night started with everyone going around the circle and giving their thirty-second elevator pitch.

"I'm Susan, I don't just sell shakes, I sell a lifestyle. I sell dreams and then I work my ass—oops, butt—off to help you achieve your dreams. Ask me how you can be an independent business owner."

"I'm Anne. I'm a mortgage broker. We're the only all-female office in the metro and we cater to single female homebuyers."

"Ha! Cater. Great segue! I'm Grace, and I'm a caterer. I'd love to help you make your next event deliciously successful."

We got to me last. I'd been hanging just outside the circle hoping I'd be skipped, because I had no idea what to say: "I'm Jen. If nothing else, at least my mom thinks I'm a big fucking deal. I'm an author. I've sold hundreds of thousands of books. I have over a million followers on social media. I travel the country entertaining crowds and I hate pants. I also may be in the midst of a midlife crisis and I bet some of you are too. I might have some answers for you and if anyone wants to talk about it, I'll be by the bar." Ha. I'd *never* use that as my intro! That would be crazy, right? Right?! I mean, never say never, though . . . No. It would be madness. I can't be *that* honest. Right?

It had already been a long process to go around the circle and I could see dozens of pairs of bored, tired eyes staring at me, so I decided to keep it short. "I'm Jen Mann. I'm a lady writer. I write funny books." I decided not to share the midlife crisis thing, because nice ladies don't talk about such things. Especially at women's empowerment networking events. "Fake it 'til you make it" was the unofficial theme of the night. No one wanted to talk about hormonal mood swings or thinning hair unless they had something to sell you for that particular infirmity.

After the introductions, the circle broke up and I found my-self holding up a wall, surveying the group. This tends to be my go-to position at parties. I'm more comfortable lurking in the shadows than I am diving right into a circle of chatting partygoers. I watched to see if anyone would start any mean-ingful conversations. Of course, I *can* make small talk, I just don't *want* to. It literally drains the life out of me. Not because I'm antisocial, but because I'm antibullshit. My feeling is if you want to connect with people, cut the fucking small talk. Please, stop talking about the fucking weather.

As I've aged, I've noticed that I have very little patience for anyone who doesn't have real conversations or real relation-ships with the people around them. These days I'm all about quality over quantity. We all should be. Imagine how much better your day would be if it wasn't filled with mindless con-versations. How many times have you talked about the weather, how busy you are, or how you can't find a good work-out and/or diet to follow? How many times have you listened to someone else brag about their kids or worry about how they'll pack everything they need to take for Spring Break? "Sometimes I think it's just easier to stay home, Jen!"

Uh-huh. I hope the airline loses your luggage, Susan.

Meaningful conversations don't have to be daunting. Some-times people rely on small talk because they fret over what to say to a stranger. They make boring-ass chitchat because they're worried they have nothing else to talk about and then it will get real awkward real fast. "Sooo . . . do you like . . . stuff?" But that's not true. Everyone has something they like talking about. Something they're passionate about.

As I've told you earlier, people (myself included) love to talk about themselves. And the conversation can be interesting and important, if they are being honest. As a writer, I love to hear people's stories, because often they inspire me, teach me something, or give me an idea of who that person is and what makes them tick. Everyone is an expert on something, you just need to figure out what that something is. Answers to a few well-intentioned questions can reveal a whole lot about a person.

I once met a man while waiting on line to board a plane. I'm not a big talker in those kinds of situations. I don't remember what he said to engage me in conversation, but I know I asked why he was headed to Ohio. That was all the opening he needed. The next thing I knew we ended up sitting together, and before that plane landed, I was thoroughly educated on Hamvention, one of the world's largest conventions for amateur radio operators. I had no idea the world of ham radio was so interesting or that I was sitting next to one of the celebrities of that world! When in doubt, ask an open-ended question that isn't weather-related—unless you're talking to Al Roker.

I've heard people say they don't want to open up too much because they're worried they might tread into offensive or uncomfortable territory. Yes, of course, you should keep your ass away from offensive conversations, but uncomfortable ones aren't bad. I would argue that maybe if we had more uncomfortable, reasonable, fact-based conversations with one another we wouldn't have so many angry, divided, and hurting people in this world right now. If we had uncomfortable conversations rather than burying them deep inside us, or running from them, or canceling people from our lives, or engaging in conversations only with those who are in our same echo chamber, we might be able to solve some serious shit.

That's why now every time someone asks me, "What's new, Jen?" I reply, "Well, I'm in the throes of a midlife crisis right now and it really fucking sucks."

It's always interesting to see how people respond. Some women mumble lame platitudes or say "But why? Your life is great!" and then get the hell away from me as fast as they can. But a lot of women settle in to talk and to share their own feelings.

I met Mary when I was helping Carla clean up after her event.

Mary is married to a well-known businessman. She is attractive and interesting and funny. She lives in a gorgeous home and goes on luxury vacations. Her Instagram is one of those accounts where all her photos are stunning selfies or pictures of her gorgeous children or her pampered pooch. They're curated to be in the same color scheme, and hers all have a peach hue.

"Carla says you're having a midlife crisis," she whispered, like it was a dirty little secret.

I stopped stacking chairs. "Yes, I am," I replied.

"I think I am too," she confessed quietly. "I feel like I've lost my spark."

I nodded. "I understand completely."

"But then I feel guilty! Look at my life! Everyone thinks it's so perfect. I have so much. I'm so blessed. I can't tell anyone, because my friends would judge me. But they have no idea what I'm dealing with!"

"They're probably feeling the same way, but they're afraid you'll judge them," I said. "Have you tried talking to them? Talking to my friends and family has helped me so much."

"No. Maybe it's easier for you since you're an oversharer. I follow you on Facebook. You really have no subject that's off-limits, do you? You just say whatever comes into your head," Mary said. I took that as a compliment, even though it probably wasn't meant to be one. Mary continued, "I'm a private person. I don't like to share my business with everyone."

"I'm not asking you to write a book about your feelings or talk about your menopause symptoms," I joked. "I'm just saying you should find someone to talk to."

"I don't think anyone would understand," Mary said.

"You'd be surprised," Carla said, joining us.

Mary said nothing. Carla and I stood there staring at her expectantly, waiting for her to say something. We were ready to listen. We'd literally just said we understood, and yet Mary was still reluctant to open up and share with us. Instead, she left to take a phone call that I'm pretty sure she faked. Who answers their phone anymore?

Mary assumed I put everything on social media, but she was wrong. Before I wrote my midlife crisis blog post, unless it was outrage I was feeling, I kept my emotions to myself for far too long. I let them simmer beneath the surface, and like Mary, I was afraid to share them. I was worried that people might think I was a whiner or that I'd be perceived as fragile. Keeping it all bottled up and to myself was one of the worst things I could have done. That only made me feel worse. I didn't start to feel better until I started talking.

Now I talk to my husband. I talk to my family. I talk to my friends. I talk to strangers on the Internet. And even strangers on planes. Now that I've started talking, I won't shut up. I talk to anyone who will listen. And I don't talk about the fucking weather anymore.

Some people are better than others to talk to. My friends get it. They understand exactly where I'm coming from and they are good listeners and they're always full of great advice.

My mom, not so much. Normally my mom and I get along really well, and I rely on her a lot for advice and counseling. But this is an area where she's not much of a help to me. My mom and I are very different. She doesn't like uncomfortable conversations and will avoid them at all costs. She relies on her faith a lot too. "Have you prayed about it, Jen?" is almost always the first question I get from her when I tell her I'm struggling with something. While I think there is definitely a place for faith in my life, sometimes I'd just like my mom to open up more.

I know she went through her own shit show in her forties. I was leaving for college and she freaked out. "What will I talk to your dad about?" she said. "We have nothing in common anymore!"

At the time, eighteen-year-old me thought that was the strangest thing I'd ever heard. To me, it appeared my parents were happily married. They'd been married for twenty years! How could unhappy people be married for twenty years? How could she think they had nothing in common? I laughed her off and went on my merry way.

Recently I asked her about this. "How did you and Dad get through your midlife shit?" I asked. "When I went to college and no one was around anymore?"

She waved it off like it was no big deal. "Oh, it was fine. You just get through it," she said, ending our conversation. I mean, they're still married, so I couldn't argue that her advice didn't work, but it still sucked balls.

I know a lot of people feel that they have no one to talk to, and I want to say again, loudly for the people in the back, *that's not true*. There are lots of organizations, groups, clubs, networks, message boards, syndicates, and girl gangs out there. You just have to find your people. They're not going to send you an engraved invitation, so you're going to have to do something brave and ask them if you can sit at their lunch table. But you can do it. I have confidence in you!

A few months ago, I noticed a lot of my friends were posting raw, honest, heartfelt, personal status updates that were falling on deaf ears. None of their friends were commenting or even acknowledging they'd seen the posts.

After years of managing online groups and pages, I know how many people out there just want to be seen and heard. They want to know someone cares. So I began asking a simple question on my personal Facebook page once a week: HOW ARE YOU?

The first time I asked it, I thought I'd get a lot of "Fines" and "Okays." I was surprised to see the answers that poured in. The women (and even a few guys) who follow me were hungry to have real, honest conversations where they could open up about their feelings.

"I'm in a bad place. I lost my job this week and I'm worried I won't find another one."

"Better than I was a month ago."

"I'm feeling unfocused and I have too much to do."

"I'm pissed off at the world. It infuriates me. And I'm mad at myself for caring so deeply when no one else does."

"I'm good. Still teleworking and enrolled to go back to school today. Feeling hopeful."

"I don't have cancer. So I'm thankful today."

But it wasn't just a place where they dropped their grievances and moved on. I watched as other women came along and liked or hearted their posts. They encouraged one another and cheered one another up. They offered advice, a sympathetic ear, or just a virtual hug.

The other thing that surprised me was how many of them thanked me for asking.

"No one ever asks how I am and actually cares."

"You're the first person to ask me that this week. Thank you."

"That felt good. Thanks for asking!"

And so many of them returned the favor and asked, "How are *you*, Jen?"

The endless loop of small talk will be the death of us all. Okay, maybe I exaggerate, but you know what I mean. It's just fucking awful. I don't have time to dilly-dally. Haven't you heard? I'm getting older by the second and I'm not messing around with the bullshit shallow stuff anymore. It's not healthy and I don't want it in my life. To grow and to move forward, we must connect with people on a deeper level.

It's not that hard, you just have to ask "How are you?" and mean it and make sure you have the time to hear the answer.

JEN'S GEMS

When it comes to meaningful conversations, you can never go wrong when you pick quality over quantity. No one is boring if you give them a chance and if you're willing to let your guard down too. If you're uncertain how to start, simply ask someone, "How are you?" But be ready, when they say "I'm fine," to ask again. "No. How are you, really?" That's when shit gets real.

Self-Care Is the Shit

Making Yourself a Priority

There has been a lot of talk in the last few years about self-care. Every time I open social media or email, I'm inundated with yet another headline screaming at me about the importance of self-care:

- What's Your Self-Care Routine, Moms?
- Fifty Ways Boomers Can Practice Self-Care!
- Self-Love IS Self-Care! (Mind Blown!)
- Look Out, Ladies, Self-Care for Men Is a Thing Now!
- Pamper Your Pooch with These Easy Self-Care Ideas for Dogs!

Self-care is obviously an incredibly clickable buzzword, but what does it mean, really?

When I posed the question "What do you do for self-care?" to my online community, I heard the usual from them: meditation, yoga, running, nature, spa treatments. I even heard a few unusual answers like bubble baths, rage and/or comfort baking, hanging out with friends, knitting, Netflixing, wine. Many of them told me they view self-care as a way to decompress after a stressful day or a long week. Several women use self-care as a time to focus solely on themselves and to recharge their battery.

"I need my daily run," Charlotte, forty-two, wrote. "I will run when it's blistering hot outside or when it's freezing cold. Nothing will stop me. Yes, I run for my health, but I don't even care about the physical benefits. It's all about the mental health benefits. It's the one hour when I am completely solo. I don't run with a friend, because I want to be alone with my thoughts. I am not responsible for my family or my job or anything else. It is the only 'me time' I get the whole damn day, and I protect it fiercely. My husband knows I will be a much better wife and mother if I can get my run in, so he supports me fully."

Annabelle, forty-nine, is a teacher. She wrote, "If I've had a particularly stressful day in the classroom, I stop at the grocery store on the way home so I can buy the ingredients I need to bake a cake. Eating cake will make me feel better. I could buy a cake, but I will feel better if I make the cake. Beating the batter makes me happy."

When I thought about my own self-care routine, very few of the ideas that the Midlife Bites group offered appealed to me. No surprise there, I guess. But I've been told over and over again by the media, my friends, half of the damn inspirational memes on the Internet, and even the lady behind the counter at the bakery (when I buy a pie from her for the second time in a week) how important self-care is when you're struggling. So I knew I needed to at least attempt some of these things, no matter how unappealing they sounded. If nothing else, I figured I'd check out some of their self-care ideas and write about them, because what's funnier than the idea of me trying to master the Child's Pose without farting or running without a serial killer chasing me or trying to bake bread from scratch without being pissed off that all I did was trash my kitchen and make something inedible?

I started with yoga. Several years prior, I'd gone to a yoga class with my friends Allison and Meghan. Allison had been raving for months about how yoga had changed her life. We were at one of my few favorite self-care activities: happy hour. "I'm taller, I'm leaner, I'm more grounded," she gushed. "You would love it, Jen."

I did want to be taller, leaner, and more grounded, but I'm also a chicken shit. The whole yoga thing is incredibly intimidating. It's not just a hobby, it's a goddamn *lifestyle*. There are clothes and accessories you need in order to practice the craft seriously. The yoga studios are typically full of perfectly coiffed and attired women drinking green juice from trendy sustainable and/or recyclable branded containers. I couldn't just roll into the yoga studio carrying a Diet Coke and wearing the Walmart brand "yoga" pants I'd slept in the night before. I imagined the looks I'd get when I announced I could no longer reach my toes. "I know! What the fuck, right? I'm short as hell. It's not that far. But I can't force my body to bend against its will!" Nope. I couldn't do it. And who would I hang out with? I'm brave, but the idea of showing up for a yoga class alone terrified me. Ugh. But I wanted that life-changing shit Allison was selling! I took a deep breath, called Meghan, and persuaded her to go with me to a beginner class the following week.

No surprise, it did not go well.

I did breeze into the studio sporting my Walmart "yoga" pants, but I had the sense to leave my Diet Coke in the car. The instructor greeted Meghan and me warmly and thanked us for making ourselves a priority. When I confided that I was concerned we'd make asses of ourselves, she assured me we were in a safe space and everyone was welcome and no one could do wrong in her studio.

And yet I managed to do a lot of wrong.

It was like kindergarten all over again. First, I found out quickly that it is poor etiquette to walk on someone's mat. Actually, first I found out it was poor etiquette to ask if you could *borrow* someone's mat. I didn't have my own and the Hubs wasn't thrilled with me buying shit that I'd probably never use again. So earlier that week I asked Allison if I could borrow her mat.

"Ew. No, Jen," she said, turning up her nose.

"But I'll wipe it down with disinfecting wipes when I'm done," I promised.

"Jen, you know how I feel about wipes," Allison said.

Allison had been lecturing me for years against the evils of disinfecting wipes and how they hurt the environment, but they're so handy! "Fine. I'll bleach it or whatever you want me to do," I said.

"Just bring a towel with you," Allison sighed. "Why do you have to make everything so complicated, Jen?"

"It's a gift."

So I had my beach towel rolled up and tucked under my arm when I stepped on someone else's mat. In my defense, it was the most direct route to where I needed to go and I just grazed the corner of the lady's mat, but she acted like I had infected it with leprosy. I apologized profusely, but the damage was done and now everyone was looking at me like I had fucking cooties.

I got into even bigger trouble for talking too much to Meghan. It's just that when I'm working out with a friend, half the fun is talking to that friend. It makes the time go by faster and it helps me not focus so much on the pain I'm enduring. I don't get it. This studio offered Vinyasa yoga, power yoga, hot yoga, prenatal yoga, aerial yoga, and chair yoga, but they couldn't offer one yoga class where you can chitchat the entire time? I think the owner is missing out on a million-dollar idea right there.

The only positive thing I can say about the yoga class I took is that I didn't fart or pee myself, and afterward Meghan and I got drinks as a reward for enduring that particular nightmare. Other than that, it was depressing because my life did not instantly change as promised, so no need to ever go back.

Cut to my latest self-care journey when I'd decided to give yoga another try. It was more of a self-care-necessity thing than a self-care-mood thing. I spend most of my days hunched over a computer fighting with Internet trolls, and that can wreak havoc on my back and hips, and that whole not-being-able-to-touch-my-toes thing started out as a joke but became a real problem. After spending a fortune on a chiropractor who didn't do squat, I took the advice of a friend and started doing gentle yoga stretches every morning and every evening. Once I could touch my toes again, I realized I didn't hate yoga, I just didn't love it. But since I didn't hate it and I could see results, I figured maybe I could splurge on a real mat and try some new moves. Don't get excited and be like, "Oh my god, Jen! That's like real growth for you! I'm so proud of you." It's not like I attend a class regularly or anything, because that would require my putting on a bra and pants, leaving my house, and making mindless small talk with people about the weather.

Instead, I found Yoga with Adriene, a YouTube channel that doesn't make me feel stupid. I like Adriene a lot (look at me talking about her like we're friends or something when we've never met) and I can follow along when I want to and skip the videos I don't want to do. It's a lot of bending and stretching with a few harder moves thrown in so I have something to work toward. Physically, I feel a thousand times better. I am not as rigid with my "workout" as the runner, Charlotte, so some days I miss my "me time," which my hips are fully aware of.

I can't say that yoga's done anything for my brain, though. In fact, during those thirty minutes, I'm typically working through my to-do list and counting down the time until I can be done. If I didn't see any physical benefits to it, I probably would have quit ages ago.

I was still trying to figure out what to do for my brain when it occurred to me that mediation seems like a natural fit. Confession: Meditation blows chunks for me, but my husband loves it! He meditates every morning. He says when he's finished, his mind feels organized and clear and he's prepared to conquer the day.

For months I'd been complaining that my brain felt like mashed potatoes and the Hubs had been begging me to try meditation, which I finally agreed to. We lay on the floor of our bedroom and closed our eyes and he started the meditation app on his phone. The sounds of an overactive rain forest filled the room.

"Is this it?" I asked. "Just rain forest noises? What am I supposed to do with that?"

"That's the intro," the Hubs said. "Just wait."

The lady on the app started speaking, telling us to close our eyes and let her guide us on our journey toward peace, tranquility, and self-discovery or some shit like that. I actually have no idea what she said, because I quit paying attention almost immediately. I was completely thrown off by her voice. "What's that accent?" I asked the Hubs.

"Shhh," he said.

"Is it Irish or Scottish? It's kind of hard to concentrate with her talking, right?"

"Shhh! Listen to her. She's telling you what to do."

"Oh wait, no, I'm pretty sure she's Australian. Her accent threw me for a minute," I said.

"Shhh!"

I sat up and poked the Hubs. "Hey, how long does this last?"

The Hubs opened one eye and glared at me. "Jen!"

"Well, it's just that I have a lunch today. I don't want to be late."

He closed his eyes and tried to go Zen. "It's eight in the morning, Jen. You have plenty of time to get to your lunch."

"Right. But I need to shower . . . and . . . get dressed . . . do my hair . . ."

The Hubs breathed deeply. "You'll be fine."

I assumed my meditation position again, eyes tightly closed, and tried to concentrate. *Come on, Jen, focus your mind and meditate, you dummy!* "Is that the sound of waves in the background now? What happened to the rain forest? That's annoying, right?" Interesting tidbit about me: The sound of ocean waves grates on my nerves. I do not find that sound peaceful and I could never live near the beach. Well, I guess I could if my house was soundproof. I like to *look* at the ocean, but I don't like to *hear* it. The Hubs remained silent, but I could feel irritation radiating from him in waves. Ugh. Even more waves.

I listened closer. "Hang on. Nope. It's not waves, it's wind. Hmm, is the sound of wind making you feel chilly, or is just me? Now I might need a blanket."

The Hubs sat up and snapped at me, "Oh my god, shut up, Jen, shut up and fucking meditate already!"

"So crabby," I whispered. "I thought this meditation shit was supposed to make you calm. Sheesh."

Spoiler alert: That was my one and only attempt at meditation.

Running will never be my thing either. I don't run. I lumber. I hobble along. I think "runner's high" is hashtag fake news. Basically, if you see me running, you'd better run too, because shit is going down. I will be the first to be eaten in a zombie apocalypse. You're welcome. No amount of coercion or pleas will get me to even try running as part of my self-care journey.

Every day on Facebook, my friend Elise posts a screenshot of her running map. When I look at the outline from her runs all I see is food. Sometimes it looks like she ran a doughnut. Sometimes I see a chicken leg. Once I saw a Hershey bar. When I showed the Hubs, he said, "Jen, her neighborhood is a grid. That's just a rectangle." I don't know. I saw chocolate.

My neighbor Ingrid walks every day. I know, because every time I leave my house she's out for a stroll. Never once has Ingrid put up her map on Facebook and been like, "Walked three miles! Boom! Bitches get it done!" But my runner friends always let me know they've gone for a run while I sat around watching Netflix like it's my job. I get it, though. If I worked out, I'd announce it on social media too. I'm denying myself carbs and sugar, I need to feel love somehow! Likes and heart emojis will have to suffice. Ingrid should put up her map. Maybe it would look like a wedge of cheese to me.

So far, I'd struck out on the self-care suggestions, but then I remembered spa day was on there.

Yes. Spa days are something I can totally get behind. Especially now that I'm older. I used to be self-conscious at the spa and I never quite knew the proper etiquette for the various treatments. One of the first times I went for a massage, my brain went into overdrive with all of these questions—Do I leave my panties on? Did I shave my legs recently enough? Can I eat the cucumber slices covering my eyes?

As I've aged, I've learned to embrace spa day and just be myself and revel in the pampering. I've been to some really nice spas all over the world, and no matter where I was, I noticed that the vibe in the locker room was always the same. I saw women of every age, rocking every body type, in every stage of dress or undress, and showcasing every kind of grooming technique. I realized that none of these ladies gave a fuck at the spa. Everyone in that room was paying hundreds of dollars to be there and they were going to enjoy their damn selves however they wanted. Meanwhile, I, too, had spent hundreds of dollars to be there and I was in a corner fretting over the fact that I didn't properly shave my big toe hair before I arrived. What a waste of energy and money!

Once I gave in to the experience and let go of my worries, though, spa days quickly became my go-to form of self-care.

Every holiday, birthday, anniversary, Arbor Day, whatever, my family asks, "What do you wa—"

"Spa day!"

Yeah, spa days (or even spa hour) can be great, but who can afford to go more than once or twice a year?

There had to be other kinds of self-care things that I could try. And that I would like.

I tried to think about what made me feel good. Besides chocolate, salt, and liquor, there's reading, writing, and napping.

When I told my friend Karen about my ideas of self-care, she said, "I get the whole food and booze thing, but reading, writing, and napping?"

Are you kidding me right now? Reading is the best! It has been my escape hatch my entire life. Bad day at school? Curl up with a murder mystery and (virtually) kill off all your enemies. Mom and Dad want you to clean your room? Hide in the closet and escape to Narnia instead. No date (again) for Valentine's Day? A good rom-com (or erotic fiction if you need something a bit stronger) will scratch that itch!

Reading calms my mind, relaxes me, and, bonus, it helps me be a better person. Seriously. Everything I read teaches me something. I'm not bragging about reading a lot of deep shit, but if you open your mind you can learn all sorts of things no matter what you're reading. Most writers are telling their own stories and teaching you about their lives and their experiences. Reading an assortment of books and genres helps me be more empathetic and open-minded, which I admit is not always easy.

And while reading is great, writing is even better for my

own self-care. While I've never been the type of person to keep a daily journal, I've always been a storyteller. As a kid I wrote down the stories of my life in spiral notebooks and squirreled them away in the back of my closet. It wasn't until I hit my thirties and learned about blogging that I really got serious about writing as a form of self-care. I had so much to say but felt I had no one to say it to. I started a blog to write down my feelings and my opinions, but I never had any idea my self-care would turn into a career. That was just a lucky break for me. Now that writing is my job, I sometimes get stressed out by my J-O-B. That's why I still write, but for myself. I have a shit ton of work that no one's ever seen and probably never will see. I vent my spleen and pour out my heart and brain on the page and then I feel so much better. I feel less angry and lighter and not as overwhelmed. A lot of times when I have something important to say to the Hubs or my kids I will write it down first, because it's hard for me to get my thoughts in order otherwise.

Now let's talk about my absolute favorite form of self-care: napping. Because napping is the greatest thing ever. When I was in high school my dad quit his corporate job to start his own company. He worked from home and every afternoon around one o'clock he'd take off his shoes and lie down on the couch for a quick nap. He didn't nap long. Maybe thirty or forty minutes. We teased him about needing a warm bottle too, but he wasn't having it. "I need a break!" he said. "My brain and my body are tired and I'm going to take a few minutes." He woke up refreshed and ready to tackle the rest of the day. Meanwhile, back in those days my mother was a stay-at-home mom who did everything for our family. Her job was seven days a week, twenty-four hours a day. When she wasn't cooking, cleaning, or shuttling my brother and me around town, she was cooking and cleaning some more. I never saw my mom take a nap. Guess which one of my parents complains about stress and which one doesn't?

And it's not just my parents, my ninety-five-year-old grandmother swears the secret to her long life and good health can be boiled down to a few key things. Touch your toes, go for a walk, read the Bible, and take a nap every day. Now that I've hit middle age, I finally understand her wise words—especially the napping bit. I've figured out that my magic number is one hour. When I am struggling to get work done or I'm feeling overwhelmed, I set an alarm on my phone and climb under my covers for a quick recharge. Thirty minutes isn't long enough—I wake up grumpy and irritated I didn't get a "good" nap—and ninety minutes is too long—I feel like I got hit by a bus and I can't remember my name or what day it is. If I accidentally nap for ninety minutes, I might as well just go back to sleep for the long haul because there's no coming back from that nonsense.

As self-care became a hot buzzword, it also produced a strong backlash. We are known for tearing down popular shit. I've seen countless op-eds calling self-care "selfish" and "entitled" and a "luxury." I get it. Not everyone has the money for daily yoga classes, a spa day, or a girls' trip to Turks and Caicos. A lot of women feel they don't even have time for a nap every day. Okay, I hear you, but I think you're wrong. There's always time to do something relaxing for yourself. Self-care doesn't need to be expensive unless you want it to be. It's all about priorities and making yourself one of them.

For instance, you could skip cleaning your sink or binge-watching the hot new Netflix show and go to bed earlier one night a week. You could turn off your phone for half an hour and go for a walk or (gasp) a run. You could take a hot bath or a long shower. You could write down your thoughts in a notebook during your lunch hour. You could download a guided meditation app on your phone or watch yoga videos on YouTube and try that shit out for yourself instead of watching mindless TikTok videos. You could turn up the music really loud and shake your ass. You could close the door and sit in your silent bedroom and be alone with your thoughts.

If you're like me, your family is probably a great cause of the stress in your life, but if you don't tell them, they'll never know. You have to ask for help (not scream that you're literally dying and could someone please do just one fucking thing on your to-do list). You have to ask nicely and clearly state what you want because no one is going to just offer it willingly. You have to let them know that you're making yourself a priority so that you can be a better wife, mother, daughter, etc. It's been said a million times, but let me be the one to say it one million and one times: We women have to put our oxygen masks on first. If your spouse or family members love you, then it should not be a problem to ask for and receive support. Charlotte's husband understands how important her daily run is to her and to their relationship, so he's happy to see her jog out the door. Allison's family knows that Saturday mornings are for yoga and they try not to complain when she heads out for an hour or so. When I'm showing signs of stress, the Hubs is always the first to say, "I think you need to go write about this."

Self-care doesn't need to be expensive or a huge time suck, but it does have to be whatever you need it to be. Of course, I'm not advocating for anything illegal or harmful to your

health or relationships, but I am saying everyone needs to figure out what it is that makes them feel better and do more of it.

JEN'S GEMS

Spoiler alert: Self-care is whatever the fuck you
want it to be. Take a bath, go for a walk, read a
book, pet a dog, solve a cold case, rage craft, de-
molish your master bathroom, eat pie, scream into
a pillow. It doesn't matter what you do as long as
it's legal and it makes you feel better. And remember, don't feel bad about doing it. You deserve it!

Why Are My Eyes Such Dicks?

Staying on Top of Your Health

I was a fairly healthy middle-aged woman before my eyes staged a revolution. When I say healthy, I mean my blood pressure was low and I could run a mile if someone was chasing me with a knife. I was as healthy as an overweight woman without diabetes or any other major ailment could be. So I was more than a little surprised when the pain in my eye woke me up before my alarm.

"Ow," I muttered as I rubbed my eye. My eye felt swollen, and the pain intensified when I put any pressure around my eye socket. "What the hell?"

I scrambled out of bed and headed for the bathroom. When I turned on the light I could see that something wasn't right with my eye. Besides the swelling, it was an angry bright red and tearing up. The light stung horribly and caused my eye to tear even more. I put my hand carefully over my eye to shield it from the bright bulb. I turned off the overhead light and tried to get a closer look in the mirror with just the natural light streaming through the bathroom window. It was barely dawn, the daylight wasn't bright, but my eye was still sensitive to it. I could, however, at least open it for a closer examination. Once the eye was open, it hurt even more. Every time I blinked it was like the underside of my eyelid was covered in sandpaper. The pain from the light and the blinking hurt so much I was ready to bawl.

"Is everything okay?" the Hubs asked. He was still in bed and trying to look concerned, but I knew he just wanted to go back to sleep.

"My eye is messed up," I said. "I think I need to see a doctor or something."

Three of the four people in my family wear glasses, so we all see an eye doctor every year. But we go to that eye doc in a box at Costco. That guy was fine for figuring out our prescription lenses, but would he know what to do with my mystery eyeball? Plus, it was a Sunday. I didn't think he'd be in on a Sunday and there was no way I could wait until Monday. The pain was unbearable.

I used my one good eye and scrolled through Google until I found an emergency optometrist who would see patients on demand. I called the number and left a message explaining my symptoms. Within a few minutes, I received a call back. I answered a few general health questions and then I was given an appointment.

A few hours later I was in a dark room with a doctor who examined my eyes and asked if anything unusual had happened to my eyes recently.

"Unusual?" I asked, confused.

"Do you recall being poked by anything sharp?" he asked.

"In my eye?" I said.

"Yes."

If that had happened, I think I would have started my emergency call to his office with that tidbit of information. I'm not one to bury the lede. "No," I said.

"Maybe not sharp, then. Just a jab in the eye," he said.

That's when I remembered that I'd taken my kids to the pool two days before. We had a water gun fight and Gomer was getting quite competitive, as twelve-year-old boys tend to do. I had him pinned in a corner and I was blasting him but my gun ran out of water. I called a truce to refill, but instead of honoring our agreement, he saw a chance to ambush me. He fired a stream of water that got me directly in the eye. The same eye that was now on fire.

"Ahhh," the doctor said, nodding. "I thought I saw a scratch on your cornea but I couldn't be sure. Now it makes sense. You have a scratched cornea. Take these drops four times a day for two or three days until your eye feels better and you'll be back to normal."

It all seemed so simple and easy. I tried not to think too much about how uncertain the doctor had been regarding my diagnosis just a few minutes before but now suddenly had an answer. The scratched cornea made sense. It was a common problem, and I *had* taken a painful direct hit in the eye.

I paid my bill, took my drops, and headed home. I thought that would be the end of it. Little did I know that I would spend the next two and a half years trying to figure out what exactly was wrong.

Initially, my eye cleared up, just as the doctor promised. I stopped the drops, and within a week my eye flared up again and this time was worse because instead of just the one eye, now both of my eyes were affected. I called the doctor who had diagnosed me and he had me come back to the office.

"What did you do to this eye?" he asked.

"Nothing," I replied. "Is that cornea scratched too?"

He peered into my eyes and then he rolled his chair over to his computer. He typed something in the computer and then said, "Did I say your cornea was scratched?"

"Yes. A couple weeks ago."

"Hmm. Well, I was wrong. It wasn't scratched. It couldn't have been. Because now you have a virus."

"A virus? Like pinkeye or something?"

"Exactly. You had a virus when you came in before, but the inflammation made it difficult to ascertain. I assumed it was a scratched cornea, but it's clearly a virus."

"How do you know?"

"Because it's jumped to the other eye now. You need to take extra precautions. You could give this virus to everyone in your family if you aren't careful."

He sent me home with more eye drops and strict orders to wash my sheets and towels daily and no hugs or kisses until further notice.

As I was paying yet another bill to him, he asked, "Do you wear makeup?"

"Of course," I said.

"Throw it all out. The brushes too."

"I have hundreds of dollars tied up in that shit," I said.

He shrugged. "You'll just keep reinfecting yourself."

The eye drops worked for a few weeks, but when I woke up with my eyes swollen shut I found another doctor.

"You're sure the cornea wasn't scratched?" the new doctor asked.

"I'm positive. If it was scratched and I've been on all this medication for a month now, wouldn't it be healed?"

He didn't like hearing that. He also diagnosed a virus. But a different one than the first guy.

The third doctor took a little more time with me. By that point, my eyes had been fucked up for close to six months. Between the constant fogged vision and the sensitivity to light, I couldn't see or do anything. I was in constant pain, and my vision was so blurry I could barely read or type. I couldn't do much except sit in a dark room and cry. I wasn't getting a diagnosis or treatment plan for my illness and I was sinking into a depression. And even though the medication had worked at the beginning, my eyes were no longer responding to it. Nothing was working.

My third doctor decided to run blood tests and see if I had any of the usual suspects that cause eye drama: diabetes, cataracts, macular degeneration, glaucoma. And the unusual suspects: lupus, multiple sclerosis, Lyme disease, and more.

He gave up on me when my blood work came back normal. He shrugged his shoulders and said, "Yeah, I don't know what to tell you."

Fuck! I was only forty-five years old and my body was revolting on me and now three doctors had been like, "Sucks to be old."

I was on my fourth eye doctor when I got some hope. He examined my eyes and ruled out a tumor or anything visible. That's when he mused out loud, "Probably not syphilis. Surely someone tested you for that." He thumbed through the stack of paperwork I'd brought with me.

I about came unhinged. *Fucking syphilis? Seriously? That's your bright idea?* But still I held my breath while he read my file. Because as much as I wanted a diagnosis, syphilis was definitely, definitely not the one I hoped for.

"Nope. You tested negative for that."

Phew. Thank God.

"Well, it looks like you have a standard uveitis," he said, shrugging.

I was used to the shrug, but "uveitis" was a new word to me.

"Wait. What's that?" I asked.

"Uveitis? It's just inflammation in the eyes. It's usually caused by rheumatoid arthritis."

"Arthritis?" I asked. Isn't arthritis an old person disease? My grandmothers had arthritis. "I don't have arthritis."

"Well, maybe not in your hands or knees, but think of it like you have arthritis in your eyes."

What the fuck kind of old lady disease was that? My grandmas had inflammation in their joints, not in their fucking eyes! *Never mind, Jen. Focus on the positive. He knows what's wrong with you. Let's make it better!* "Can you fix it?" I asked, hopefully.

He shook his head. "No. You need a specialist."

That sounded expensive. I'd already spent hundreds of dollars on doctor visits and prescriptions I didn't need, and I couldn't forgive or forget the first doctor who was convinced I had some rare virus that kept "jumping eyes" and I needed to throw out all of my makeup and brushes. I'm still pissed off at that guy because my favorite eye shadow was discontinued before I could replace it.

When I told the Hubs what the doctor said, he immediately hopped on the Internet. "There's only a couple of doctors who can treat you. I did all the research and I think you should try Dr. Mason first."

Within a few days the Hubs and I were sitting in the waiting room of Dr. Mason's office. I had a two-inch-thick manila folder on my lap. It contained all of my medical records, every note I'd taken after my appointments, a list of all the medications I'd tried, and a detailed timeline of my flare-ups.

I was prepared to hand over the folder when the nurse handed me a stack of paper as thick as my file. "They told you this is a three-hour appointment?" she asked.

I nodded. Every doctor up until that point had spent maybe twenty minutes with me, so I was surprised that Dr. Mason needed so much time. "Why is it so long?" I asked.

"Well, first you need to fill out all of this paperwork. It's a detailed family history and more. And then Dr. Mason will go over all of it with you and ask you even more questions. And then the exam alone will take him an hour at least. Do you need a pen?"

I handed the paperwork to the Hubs because I couldn't see well enough to fill it in. He read the questions out loud. "Have you or any member of your close extended family ever been bitten by a rattlesnake?" he asked.

"Does it ask that?" I asked, shocked.

He laughed. "No, but practically. He wants to know if your parents, your grandparents, or your great-grandparents had hypertension. He wants to know if you hike in the woods or have any unusual hobbies like foraging for wild mushrooms or berries. He wants to know if we have an open marriage!"

"I was negative for syphilis," I said. "He can rule that out."

In my entire life, I've never had a medical history questionnaire like Dr. Mason's. After answering all of his questions, we turned in the paperwork and waited for my name to be called.

I was finally ushered into a dim office. Tools and lenses littered the desk. Posters detailing the anatomy of the eye hung on the walls. And a small, rotund man sat on a stool in the middle of the room. He was going through my paperwork and didn't even glance up when we entered the room. He continued to read silently, and occasionally he'd ask for clarification on some of my answers.

"Why did so many doctors think it was a scratched cornea?" he asked.

"I don't know," I said. "I got hit in the eye with water."

"No, that won't do it," Dr. Mason said. "That was a coincidence."

"Because they were lazy," the Hubs said. The Hubs was sick and tired of me being sick and tired and he was not impressed with any of the doctors I'd seen thus far.

"Hmm," Dr. Mason said. He put down the papers and turned to me. "Okay, let's see what's going on."

For the next two hours he ran tests and took measurements of my eyes. At one point he literally sketched a picture of my eyeballs on Post-it notes and added them to my official file. He clapped his hands and said, "Okay, okay, okay. I want to see you again in three days."

"Wait. Do you know what's wrong with her?" the Hubs asked.

"Of course," Dr. Mason said.

"Can you fix me?" I asked.

Dr. Mason patted my hand and said, "That's what I do, dear."

I know now that at first Dr. Mason thought I was a fairly simple case. I was young—easily his youngest patient—and I had no underlying medical condition that would cause this inflammation in my eyes. He was positive that with proper care I'd heal right up.

It didn't go quite that easily. At one point I was visiting his office twice a week for two- and three-hour appointments.

I joined an online support group just to make sure we were doing everything we could, and it was devastating to see how many people in the group couldn't keep their jobs. It was a vicious circle—they couldn't be away from their job for the long doctor appointments that they needed, but if they didn't get treatment, they were blind and couldn't do their job.

I was lucky because Dr. Mason had cleared up my eyes enough that I could drive myself. I could also use my laptop if I blew the font up really big. So when he was off consulting with other doctors or waiting for test results to come back, I would work.

At one point Dr. Mason teamed up with a rheumatologist, Dr. Klein. That's when things really started to change for me and I began to improve and have fewer flare-ups.

Dr. Klein didn't spend near as much time with me as Dr. Mason, but he was also a very attentive doctor who truly cared about his patients. One day I was in Dr. Klein's office and I asked about the medication I was on.

"It's working, but I think it's making my brain foggy," I said.

Dr. Klein shook his head. "No, that's not a side effect. It's really just your liver and your immune system that are affected."

"But I'm having a hard time focusing and concentrating. It all started around the same time as the medication."

Dr. Klein looked at my chart. "Yeah, and so did perimenopause."

"Huh?"

"You're probably in perimenopause. You have the classic symptoms. Muscle aches, weight gain, forgetfulness, difficulty concentrating, vaginal dryness, incontinence."

"You know I have all those symptoms?" I asked.

"Dr. Mason takes thorough notes."

"Of course," I said, nodding.

"Are you doing anything to help combat these symptoms?" he asked.

"You mean other than screaming into the void?" I asked.

He laughed. "Yes, other than that."

"Well, for the past couple years I've been pretty focused on not going blind, so raging hormones had to take a back seat to overwhelming stress."

"It's all related, actually. And there are therapies I could recommend. Or if you would like a more natural approach, we could talk about that too."

"Yeah, thanks," I said, slightly embarrassed that my ophthalmologist and my rheumatologist knew more about my lady problems than my gynecologist did.

But then I wasn't embarrassed, I was angry. I was angry that neither my primary care doctor nor my gynecologist had ever spent even half the time talking to me about perimenopause and menopause than my ophthalmologist and rheumatologist did! I don't know if this is the difference between primary care doctors and specialists or if this is the difference between bad doctors and good doctors.

All I know is that I was part of the problem too. When I was dealing with perimenopause I let one doctor's opinion about therapy sway my decision. When my gynecologist said not much could be done to treat me, I resigned myself to living with a body going through life-altering changes for the next five to fifteen years and just dealing with it. I didn't go out and look for a second opinion. I didn't ask friends and family for advice. I didn't join an online support group to learn more about my ailments. I just said, "Well, fuck, I guess this is my life now."

But when I started going blind, I didn't say, "Well, fuck, I guess I'm blind now." No! I had to advocate for my care. I went out and found doctors, and every time I was dissatisfied with the answers I was getting, I found another one and another one. I joined support groups and I read everything I could find about my illness. I wasn't prepared to stop until I found someone who could help me.

Am I cured?

No.

Can I see?

Yes.

I'm still on medication that controls the inflammation, but in addition to that I've had to make a lot of changes to my lifestyle. I was forced to cut back on my workload and manage my stress better, I do yoga every day (no meditation, though, because fuck that), and I've changed my diet, because like Dr. Klein said, "it's all related."

We still don't know what caused this to happen to me, but I am positive it's related to the fact that for years I never made myself and my health a priority. As women, we tend to do that. But we also need to put some responsibility on our doctors. Many times we put off our annual doctor visits, and then when we finally do go, our complaints are ignored or met with platitudes—"It will get better," "It's all in your head," "If you lost weight this would all disappear." We have to push back and demand better care or we need to find new doctors who will listen.

If the doctors aren't doling out head pats and bullshit, we're plied with drugs. Let me be very clear here, I'm not against drugs. I think pharmaceuticals have improved people's lives and I am a huge fucking fan of medicine. I'm talking about doctors who prescribe the wrong drugs or overprescribe. For instance, when men and women complain about pain, women have been prescribed sedatives and men have been given pain-relieving drugs. My friend Craig had a vasectomy last month. After a thirty-minute procedure, he was sent home with Oxy-Contin for his pain. My friend Selena had a baby the same week. Her doctor recommended an ice pack and some Tylenol. On the other hand, just about every woman who even remotely complains about anxiety has a ton of Xanax in her purse. Again, Xanax is a lifesaver for many people and I am thrilled it can help them, but on the flip side, many people have been overprescribed.

All of this to say, trust yourself. You know your body better than anyone. You know when something isn't right and when something isn't working. As we age, more and more things are going to go to pot, and we need to be vocal with our healthcare providers. You aren't a bother to them, you aren't a pain in the ass, you aren't a complainer, you aren't a know-it-all. You are a woman who deserves to be heard and to have her ailments taken seriously.

When I complained about my initial treatment to a good friend who is a retired doctor, she told me that in medical school she learned the expression "When you hear hoofbeats, don't look for zebras."

"Everyone thinks they're a zebra, Jen," she said.

You may not be a zebra, but you're not an old, stupid horse either, and if your doctor can't or won't listen and help you deal with your ailments, then fuck them. Find someone new. You're worth it.

JEN'S GEMS

No one else will advocate for you, so you have to speak up when you know something's wrong. Never doubt yourself. Always trust your gut. Don't be afraid to break up with doctors—there are literally a million more. And just know, sometimes you're a goddamn zebra.

I Do Everyfuckingthing

Asking for Help

We'd had our trip to Orlando planned for months when we got the news that my grandfather had passed away. He'd been quite ill for some time, so it wasn't a shock, but it was still immensely sad for all of us. The funeral was scheduled for the morning of our intended departure for Florida.

I did the math, and if we pulled the kids out of school a day earlier than we'd planned and drove three hours to Omaha the night before, we could attend the funeral in the morning and the family luncheon that was to follow, turn around, and head back down to the airport in Kansas City, getting there just in time to make our flight that night.

It meant leaving on our trip a day earlier than we'd planned. So, instead of getting my real work done, I spent the day working through my giant to-do list to get everyone ready to leave. I had to make a few calls because the kids were going to miss school, dentist appointments, and basketball practice. Bad weather was rolling in and we needed to get on the road as soon as school was out, so that meant I had to pack for myself and the kids. I'd already done all the laundry earlier in the week and told them not to put away anything they were taking on the trip. I dug suitcases out of the attic and filled them with the shorts, T-shirts, and swimsuits they'd left out. I found their toiletry bags in the bathroom and tossed those into the suitcases along with a couple more pairs of underwear for each of them, because I'd finally learned that when you're a woman of a certain age, traveling with "just enough" pairs of underwear is not a good plan. I remembered Adolpha's goggles for the pool and Gomer's favorite sweatshirt. I added in cellphone chargers, books to read in the car and on the plane, snacks, and just a few more pairs of emergency underwear. That would take care of Orlando, where the weather was going to be hot, but the weather in Omaha was going to be a bone-chilling fourteen degrees and the funeral was outside.

Gomer wears shorts every day regardless of the weather. I'll be honest, I gave up trying to convince him otherwise when he was in fifth grade. I figured there were more important things to fight with him about than shorts when all he's doing is running from my car into the school or from my car into a store. But standing outside in arctic temperatures for a forty-five-minute graveside service was not a place for shorts. I texted him.

ME: Where do you keep your pants?
GOMER: Pants?

ME: Yes, pants. Long things that cover your legs.

GOMER: On the shelf in the closet.

I went to the shelf and found two lone pairs of sweats.

ME: These are sweatpants.

GOMER: They're joggers.

ME: Whatever. You can't wear them to a funeral. Don't you have any real pants?

GOMER: No. You stopped buying them in fifth grade because I stopped wearing them.

ME: Okay. I will figure it out.

I checked Adolpha's closet. She does wear pants, but they're of the yoga variety. She had a couple of dresses, but they were all strappy sundresses. I texted her.

ME: Do you have funeral clothes?

ADOLPHA: What kind of clothes?

ME: Do you have anything black? Any pants?

ADOLPHA: I have leggings. They're black.

ME: No dress pants or anything?

ADOLPHA: Are you speaking English? What are those?

Ugh.

Adolpha had only leggings and jeans with giant holes in the knees. Neither choice was appropriate for a funeral or a glacial landscape.

After I finished packing everyone's Orlando shit I went to the store to try to find appropriate clothes for my kids to wear to a subzero funeral. All I can say is luckily, I was shopping for a funeral on my dad's side of the family. They have much lower standards and are a lot harder to offend than my mom's side. Hell, Gomer and Adolpha could probably have shown up in joggers and leggings and the only person who would have judged me would have been my mom. Adolpha wasn't too hard, but I had to guess what size pants Gomer wore. I ended up coming home with three different pairs with the idea he could try them on and when we got back from Orlando I'd return the ones that didn't fit, because I'd love to go back to the store again!

As I packed each suitcase, I placed it in the front hall for the Hubs to put in the minivan. I was packing a duffel bag full of coats, gloves, hats, and scarves for everyone when the Hubs complained, "Another bag? You have so much shit! Why do you always pack so much?"

I counted to ten and tried to control my anger. This is the fight we have every time we go on a trip somewhere. Every time we travel he complains about how much "shit" I pack. But I don't see it as packing a lot of shit. I see it as packing all the things I need and all things the kids need and even some of the things he might fucking need too. The Hubs takes about fifteen minutes to pack one tiny carry-on and then brags about how little he's taking. "Why can't you be more like me?"

Oh, I don't know, maybe because I like to wear clean clothes every day? Yeah, no matter how many days we're gone, the Hubs wears his "good outfit" on the plane and then packs one extra pair of pants or shorts (depending upon the destination weather) and two shirts. The only thing clean every day on his body is his underwear.

I don't do that. Especially if I'm going somewhere hot like Florida. The last thing I want to do is put on the same pair of pants I sullied the day before with my swampcrotch. And no matter how careful I am, every shirt gets spilled on or pitted out. By the end of the day, my socks reek and need to be retired. Hell, even my bras are all single-use.

And don't get me started on his toiletries! He throws a toothbrush in his bag and bums toothpaste off me. He uses the hotel soap and shampoo and he's the rare beast who never sweats or stinks so he doesn't even *own* deodorant. I pack my own shampoos (the curl enhancer type *and* the purple kind), conditioner, and soap because the hotel stuff trashes my delicate hair and skin. I have three face creams I use daily. I have a curling iron and a blow dryer (I don't like the hotel's blow dryer, it can't get my hair dried fast enough). I bring deodorant, powder, a razor, Q-tips, floss, tweezers, nail clippers, and Band-Aids. I can't forget my prescription meds along with Aleve, Tums, and Benadryl. And finally there is a bucket of makeup and makeup accoutrements because it takes a lot of makeup to look this fucking "natural."

He makes fun of me, but guess who uses my nail clippers and tweezers the most? Guess who needs a Band-Aid when he gets a blister on his heel because he didn't pack an assortment of shoes? Who borrows my "hair goop" because he forgot his on the bathroom counter? That motherfucker.

But when he complained about all my "shit" this time, I'd had enough. My grandfather was dead. My family was in mourning. I wanted to say goodbye to my grandpa properly and support my grandma. I was jumping through a million hoops trying to make everything work so I could make everyone happy. We would lose thousands of dollars if we called off our vacation. My dad had even moved the funeral to accommodate our schedule. My aunts and uncles and cousins had all made their plans around us. The kids were missing school and would need to make up work during their vacation. I was sacrificing my precious writing time to get all this "shit" into suitcases. I had figured out the logistics of how we could be in two places at once and how we could get all our "funeral" clothes into one bag so we wouldn't have to unpack the entire car in Omaha. I had checked the weather, and I'd lived in Nebraska before, so I knew it would be fucking frigid at the funeral and now he was nagging me because I had a bag of goddamn hats and mittens so my family wouldn't get frostbite? I silently pulled out his hat and mittens and put them back in the closet because, fuck him.

I had done everything to get ready for this trip and he had one job: loading the fucking car, and he couldn't even do that without commentary.

I had to do all the packing and running around for pants by myself because that morning the Hubs had announced that he had a very important meeting that couldn't be moved, so I was on my own to get everything done. Honestly, sometimes I prefer it, because he really sucks when it comes to that kind of stuff. But still, it irked me. Apparently my work wasn't important. It wasn't important to him that I actually get paid for what I do, that I put myself on a daily schedule to produce so many words so I can meet my contractually obligated deadline. It wasn't important to him that now that I had to spend the day doing all these other things instead of writing, I would be behind.

None of this mattered to him. All that mattered was that he's very important and he needed to go to his meeting. Fine. Whatever. Go.

I was so furious with him and the situation he put me in that I also almost set my house on fire. (I blame him for that too.)

When he left me home to pack, at some point I decided it would be a good idea to clean the oven.

Yeah, I don't know why I thought this, either. I'm going to blame it on grief and stress. Both of these emotions do strange things to people. Anyway, I was in the kitchen and I could see that the oven was a disaster. I knew Adolpha had cooked something the night before, but I had no idea what it was. The trashed oven was making me antsy. I'm not a person who needs her house clean before she leaves town. I'm not even the kind of person who needs all the dishes done before she goes to bed at night. There is always something soaking in the sink. But that oven was making me insane. Every time I went by the kitchen I could see how dirty it was. That's when I got the genius idea to run the self-clean option. It always stinks up the house when the self-clean mode is on, but if I did it now we'd be gone for the worst of it. I could hole up in my bedroom and pack my suitcase while the oven stunk up the house. We'd leave town and the house would be aired out when we got back. It was genius, really.

I hit the button and the oven went to work while I retreated to my bedroom to finish packing. About an hour later, I went to the kitchen to get a drink. That's when I saw the flames.

Tall flames were dancing around inside my oven! I realized Adolpha had made bacon the night before and she'd spilled the grease all over. That's why the oven looked so dirty! I was paralyzed as I watched the flames grow taller and more intense.

All I could think was, *My house is going to burn down because everyone in my family is a lazy asshole!*

But why was I doing all the things? My kids weren't babies anymore, my husband has arms and legs that work, so why the fuck was I doing everything? Was it them, or was it me? It was probably me, because, honestly, I hate the way they do things. No one loads the dishwasher properly. The Hubs always buys the wrong brand of cereal. Adolpha doesn't fold her clean clothes, she just shoves everything in drawers. When Gomer fixes dinner, it's either burnt or raw. Does that sound familiar to you? But hear me out: Who cares how it's done? Just be glad it is done! There's cereal in the pantry, the laundry is done, and I didn't have to plan dinner!

Okay, I thought. *Clearly, I need to let go of some of my control issues, because my oven is on fire. Going forward, everyone is doing all their own shit and I'm going to force myself to just live with the way they do it. If Gomer wants to wear shorts to a funeral, I'll allow it. It won't ruin my vacation if Adolpha forgets her goggles. The next time the Hubs needs a Band-Aid for his blisters, he can live with a boo-boo on his foot. I'm done doing all the things!* And then I was like, *That's great that you've had this awakening, Jen, and you're stepping into your power to delegate and all that good shit, but there's still a motherfucking fire in your oven!*

"Oh my god, oh my god!" I screamed. "What do I do? What do I do?" I tried to remember my seventh-grade home ec class where they taught us how to extinguish grease fires. "Do I throw flour on it or pour water? Which one makes it worse? Or am I supposed to smother it? Fuck! Why can I remember *Donde esta la biblioteca?* but not how to put out a grease fire?"

I decided flour seemed vaguely familiar so that must be right. I grabbed a bag of flour and stopped myself just before I tried to open the door because all I could think of was that scene from the movie *Backdraft* where a door would open and the fire would whoosh out. At least it was currently contained in the oven. What if I opened the door and it whooshed? *Al-*

though I could use a new kitchen, I thought. *A whooshing fire might be the answer to my prayers . . . No! Focus, Jen!*

I decided I couldn't take the chance that the fire would whoosh and that throwing flour into the raging inferno in my oven would make a bigger mess than the fire, so I put the bag back in the pantry. Meanwhile, the fire still raged. I debated turning off the oven. Ugh. It wasn't clean yet, though. No matter what, I still wanted a clean oven! I was paralyzed with indecision. *When did I get so stupid?* I wondered. I was instantly furious that the Hubs wasn't there. I was certain he would know what to do and if nothing else, I could run outside to safety while he opened the oven and got whooshed by fire. "Should I call 911?" I asked the empty kitchen. I looked at the flames again. I mean, they were big for the inside of an oven, but were they 911 big? Did I really want some hot firemen coming in my house and laughing at me for thinking my little grease fire was a real emergency? I didn't want hot firemen to laugh at me!

Suddenly, I knew who to call. I grabbed my phone and dialed.

"Hi, Jen, I'm in the car and I have Grandma with me," my mom answered. She always warns me when I'm on speaker-phone and Grandma is in the car with her so I will watch my f-bombs.

Even though I was panicked, I managed to keep it G-rated. "Mom! My fu-reaking oven is on fire! It's on freaking fire! Is that freaking normal? Is it normal for your oven to catch freaking fire?"

"Your oven is on fire? How? What were you cooking?"

"I wasn't cooking. I was cleaning it. I turned on the self-clean option and now it's on fire! Is that freaking normal?"

"It's normal if you never clean it!" Mom said.

"I never use the self-cleaning option," Grandma said. "You just need a little baking soda and white vinegar."

"Stop telling me how to clean my freaking oven! Tell me how to put out the fire!"

Both Mom and Grandma started laughing.

Listening to them laugh at me made me mad. At least hot firemen laughing at me would still be hot to look at! These two yahoos were just wasting my time and my oven was still on fire. And yes, looking back now, I can totally see the irony of calling the two matriarchs of my family for advice after complaining that women do it all. But there was a fire and I knew those bitches could get shit done.

"Mom! I'm freaking serious. The fire! It's—" I looked at the oven and I could see the flames were dying down. "Oh wait. The fire is going out by itself."

"Yes, there's not a lot of oxygen in there, so once all the crumbs and stuff are burned up, it should stop," Mom said.

I watched the flames sputter out completely and I let out a huge sigh of relief. "It's done," I said. "The fire's out."

"Okay, good," Mom said. "Because have you seen the time? You need to be on the road in an hour and you do not have time for your kitchen to burn down today."

"None of us do," Grandma said.

Ain't that the motherfreaking truth.

JEN'S GEMS

Stop doing everything and delegate. It won't be pretty, and it won't be perfect, but the world won't end and your kitchen won't catch on fire. But if your oven does catch on fire, a quick Internet search tells me that flour is *not* the way to go. Baking soda or a fire extinguisher is probably a better call. So maybe go ahead and buy a fire extinguisher right now. Better yet, send someone else to the store to buy the fire extinguisher. You're fucking busy.

Next Life, No Men

Did I Mention Relationships Take Work? (See Above)

A few years ago the Hubs and I were out to lunch together, just the two of us. We don't do "date night" very often; lunches are usually our thing. It was probably supposed to be romantic or something, and I was probably supposed to be frisky and thinking about the two of us heading back to our empty house and having a quickie in the front hall before the kids came home from school. But that was the last thing I was thinking. Instead, I was watching my husband eat. I was watching him mix his food together into one gelatinous mess and scoop it into his wet mouth, and all I could think was, *Next life, no men.*

I tried to remember the days when sitting across the table from him made my stomach flip-flop or my heart skip a beat. I tried to remember when he was romantic and funny and worked hard to woo me. I tried to remember back to when I thought his quirks were cute, but instead I thought back to that morning when I watched him brush his teeth. He's a god-damn mess when he brushes his teeth. Toothpasty drool drip-ping down his chin, spittle all over the mirror and counter. But the worst part is he tries to talk to me. He uses an electric toothbrush, so between the mouthful of suds and the buzzing of the brush, I can't hear shit. "Huh, then," he said. (That's "Hey, Jen" for those of you who don't speak toothbrush.) "Ja-fargod fasli anr capota?"

A chunk of toothpaste flew out of his mouth and landed solidly on the mirror and slowly slid down the surface.

"Goddammit," I said, "the cleaning ladies were just here yesterday!"

"Thowwy," he mumbled, spitting into the sink.

"What is so important that you can't wait until you're done brushing?" I demanded.

He tried to wipe the mirror with a piece of toilet paper but that just smudged it more and left itty bitty pieces of toilet paper clinging to the mirror. I tried not to micromanage his attempt at cleaning, but it was nearly impossible. "I wanted to know if you checked the mail yesterday," he said.

That's what he wanted to ask me? He trashed the entire sink area with his minty spray so he could find out if the mail was on the counter?

Next life, no men.

Sometimes I resent my husband. Sometimes he resents me. I have a good husband, but sometimes I dream about running away.

We both work from home. We share an office. In our base-ment. We are each other's only companion. I don't have a work wife or a work husband to complain to about my real husband. I only have him.

I wonder who he complains to about me. My male friends never complain about their wives to me, but my female friends always complain about their husbands. Why is that? Maybe men are smarter than we give them credit for and they know not to talk shit about their wife to another woman because we'll cut him.

When I told my friends my "Next life, no men" theory, some said I'm not a very nice wife. But others said I'm a goddamn saint for putting up with what I do. Do you ever look at your friends' relationships and think, *I could* never *put up with that*?

For instance, my friend Constance does not work outside the home, so her husband earns all the money. She's on a tight budget and she's required to submit all her receipts to her husband at the end of the month. She must justify everything she bought, from groceries to school supplies to a monthly coffee with me. If her husband doesn't approve of her expenses, she must reimburse "the family" (which is his passive-aggressive way of saying himself, because I don't think her ten-year-old cares if she spent five bucks on a coffee) from the "allowance" he gives her.

My head almost exploded when she explained their accounting system to me. She was upset because he'd docked her ten bucks for "overpaying" for groceries the week before.

In my head I was throwing his shit on the lawn and using my allowance to change the locks on all the doors to the house. Who did he think he was? In my humble opinion, he treated Constance like a child or an employee! The fuck I'd put up with a man like that. "But, but," I stammered, "he ate those groceries. What a piece of shit, Constance!"

"Yeah, well, your husband will only take you out to dinner when he has a coupon," Constance said.

And that's when I realized Constance was thinking the same thing I was, only about *my* husband! Ouch!

When you can put up with your own spouse's shit but you think your friends are nutjobs for living with *their* husbands, that's when you know you're with the right person. That's really what marriage vows should say, because all the romantic love and honor shit doesn't mean anything twenty years down the line when you're sleeping next to a guy who farts in his sleep and couldn't hit the hamper with his dirty underwear if you paid him. And believe me, I'm not saying I'm a peach. I'm sure he looks at me and thinks, *Wasn't she fun once? I kind of remember her being nice when we first met. And how did I not realize she couldn't cook? I just stupidly assumed all women could cook.*

If we were writing our vows today, the Hubs's would be something like, "If you leave the thermostat alone, I promise to let you warm up your cold feet on me. I promise to never raise an eyebrow when you go back for seconds on dessert. I promise to pay all the bills on time so your credit score will never be bad again. I promise to always say no when you ask me if you look older than other women. I promise to hate all the same people you hate. I promise to never beg for sex and to let you know that I'm grateful for it whenever you allow it."

My vows would say something like, "I promise to leave the thermostat at sixty-eight in the dead of winter and wear layers instead of complain. I promise to eat only at restaurants where we can use a coupon. I promise to brake slowly so as not to wear my brake pads unevenly. I promise to listen to your list of ailments and nod when you say you think you're dying but we both know you really just have the sniffles. I promise to let you choose all of our technology because I only pick 'cute' laptops, not ones that actually work well."

The Hubs saw I was lost in thought and stopped eating to ask me, "What are you thinking about?"

Without thinking, I blurted out exactly what was on my mind. "Marriage is so hard. If I ever find myself single again I won't remarry," I said.

The Hubs looked shocked and maybe even a little hurt. I was surprised by his reaction.

"Wow," said the Hubs, putting down his fork.

Uh-oh. More than hurt, he'd stopped shoveling food into his mouth. "Wait. Are you mad?" I asked.

"I don't know if mad is the word, but I definitely feel kind of shitty."

"But don't you think marriage is hard?" I asked. "Like, it's difficult for you too, right?"

"Okay, I'll admit it *can* be difficult, especially if I don't agree with you. But what do you mean you'll never remarry? What if I died tomorrow? You'd be alone for the rest of your life?"

"Yep. I've decided: next life, no men," I said.

"What?" The Hubs was horrified. He dropped his voice to a whisper. "Jen, are you a *lesbian*?"

I laughed. "No! I'm attracted to men. I'm just saying I wouldn't marry again. I mean, there would still be men in my life, if you know what I'm saying, just not a husband. I'd have a friend. With benefits. *Lots* of benefits." I winked.

"Oh, okay, wow, now I feel bad," the Hubs said, shoving his plate away from him.

Uh-oh again. Loss of appetite is a terrible sign. "Why do

you feel bad? I actually meant it as a kind of compliment," I said.

"You're basically telling me our marriage stinks," he said. "That I've ruined you for marriage."

"No!" I exclaimed. "Don't you get it? I think marriage is hard but I love *you* and I'm choosing to be married to *you*. Every day I choose to put up with your shit."

The Hubs was indignant. "Well, every day I choose to put up with yours!"

"Exactly!" I exclaimed, thinking he finally understood. "I sit here and I listen to you eat even though it makes me nauseous, I watch you slobber on the bathroom mirror, and we're literally eating lunch at this restaurant because you had a BOGO coupon. But you take my worsening mood swings in stride, you rarely complain when I buy yet another pair of black pants, and you listen to me tell you how to drive every time we're in the car even though it pushes you to the edge of insanity. But marriage is hard—especially for women—and frankly I don't want to do it again."

The Hubs was offended. He was not understanding what I was talking about. Not in the least. We stayed silent for the rest of the lunch. He did manage to get his appetite back (it was either that or the thought of wasting ten bucks on a lunch that would never be consumed). When we got home, we did not have a quickie in the hall and instead retreated to different floors of our house.

I was dismayed that I couldn't get him to understand what I was trying to convey. In my mind, I was giving him a compliment. Of course, there are some days I'm not sure I'm cut out for marriage and all the work it entails, I'd be lying if I said otherwise. But I do it because I love the Hubs. The Hubs is my person. The only human whose shit I am willing to put up with. In many ways we're very similar. We have the same dark sense of humor, and neither of us has much of a filter. We're both boring as hell and think a trip to Target counts as "date night." We hate the same people and usually agree about where to spend our time and money. But marriage is also exhausting.

It doesn't help that as much as the Hubs and I are the same, we're also incredibly different people. We're from two very different cultures and had vastly different upbringings. Over the years we've worked really hard to listen to and understand each other's point of view so we could get on the same page with our parenting styles and our relationship goals. It's still hard for me to give the Hubs everything he needs, though. He would be very happy if I were his only friend. He'd like to hang out just the two of us all day, every day. And while that may sound sweet, we already both work from home and that's more than enough togetherness for me. In fact, there are many times when I beg to go to the grocery store just to be by myself. Anything to get some alone time or to be with my friends or family to be able to think and recharge my batteries. The Hubs has a tendency to suck all the energy from me and then say I'm selfish for wanting to be alone. Okay, I'll own it. I am an incredibly selfish person. Not just because I need to be alone, but also because at times it can be hard to remember that there are two of us in this relationship. I would like to blame it on the fact that we didn't get married until we were thirty, so I had many years where I got to think only of myself. But that's not the reason. The real reason is that I'm a bossy bitch. I like things the way I like them, and compromise is a tough thing for me. The Hubs is right about one thing: We only fight when he disagrees with me. We can go weeks without a squabble, and then as soon as he contradicts me or questions something I want to do, it's go time.

Often what we fight over is the way we communicate with each other. The Hubs likes to give and receive praise for what I consider to be ordinary things. Like unloading the dishwasher.

"I just thought maybe you wanted to thank me," the Hubs said.

"For . . ."

"I unloaded the dishwasher."

I looked at the kitchen counter. Yes, the plates, cups, and silverware had been put away, but any sort of "random" item like spatulas or baking sheets or mugs were left on the counter. "There are still things that need to be put away," I said.

He waved a hand. "I don't know where those things go."

"We've lived here for fourteen years. I've never changed the drawer where spatulas go."

"Why can't you just be grateful I emptied the dishwasher? I thank you when you do the laundry."

"Yeah, because I fold it and put it away."

"Why do you always pick fights with me? Why can't you just say thank you?"

I wanted to scream, "Because you did half the fucking job!"

All of these reasons and more are why I said, "Next life, no men."

I wasn't telling the Hubs that I was done being married to him. I was saying it's hard enough being married to him and I love him and I put up with a lot of his shit (and he puts up with a lot of my shit), but I wouldn't want to do that again with anyone else.

If I found myself once more single, I couldn't imagine some new guy thinking he could just roll in and share my life. I don't want another man who wants a fucking medal for knowing where the forks go, nor would I be willing to justify my spending ten dollars at Target or be admonished for leaving the bathroom light on all day. I don't want to live with the same couch for eighteen years because we can't come to an agreement about what color the new couch should be or how much we should spend on it or where it should be positioned in the fucking living room. I don't want to share my bed with a dude who sprawls over the "center line" and snores louder than a freight train. I don't want to co-parent with anyone else. It's been hard enough to co-parent with the Hubs, and those are his biological kids. Good stepparents are hard to come by and I am guessing they're all taken.

And then I think I'm lucky because the Hubs is a really great guy and what are the odds I'd find another one?

And I'm not a rare bird. The first time I said something to my friends about never marrying again, several joined my "movement." I don't think the men out there understand that at this point in our lives, middle-aged women have no real need for a husband. A few months ago I read an article in *The Globe and Mail* that talked about how many senior Canadian men were having a hard time finding women their age to settle down with. According to the article, more than sixty-eight percent of Canadian seniors are women who are single due to divorce or widowhood. Even though the men want to marry (many for the second and third time), the women aren't interested. They don't want the tensions that come along with cohabitation. They don't want to be responsible for the physical and emotional work relationships take.

I'm seeing this trend with middle-aged women too. I know lots of women who are choosing to remain single. Many are already supporting their family, so they don't need a husband to pay the bills. They're done having kids, the baby factories are closed. Sex is easy to find. In fact, many of us are approached in the produce aisle more now than ever before. Horny silver foxes are everywhere these days!

I just want some time and space to myself, is that so wrong? I can just hear someone asking, "But won't you get lonely?"

Yes, I'd get lonely, so beyond sex, companionship would be nice. But—hear me out—I'd like him to have his own place where he can go most of the time and leave spatulas on his own counter and miss his own hamper with his dirty underwear.

My friend Lori lives separate from her serious boyfriend. "I don't need a husband to feel fulfilled," she said. "My relationship is wonderful and it's on my terms."

Statistically, the chances that I will outlive the Hubs are high, so I'm already making my Golden Girls plan. I've got several roommates lined up and I'm thinking one of those tiny house communes sounds like a nice place for us to settle down.

JEN'S GEMS

I don't care how happy couples look on social media or at the kids' soccer games, everyone's marriage is hard work, so don't think you're the only one struggling. Putting up with each other's shit is a lot of work, so make sure your partner is worth it because no one wants to waste all that time and effort on a dud.

Also, apparently men are like toddlers and need a lot of praise, so if you can, thank him for (half) emptying the dishwasher.

Put On Your Big Girl Pants and Try Something Scary

Pushing Boundaries

I met Lillian several years ago at a book signing for a mutual friend. I'd heard of her, of course, because Kansas City is not a big metropolis and Lillian is a goddamn force around here. Everyone knows Lillian because she's a talented and generous person with a passion for connecting people.

Although we're friends, we're totally different. Lillian lives on the cool, hip side of town with her hubby in her empty nest where she creates art when she's not running her own company or sitting on the board of directors of other companies. I live in the burbs where I spend my free time sweating my ass off at Gomer's baseball games and buying my art at TJ Maxx. Lillian is outgoing and social. She's the type of woman who throws dinner parties and I'm the type of woman who never gets invited to dinner parties. Lillian is a fashionista who's always put together and looks like she came straight from a modeling gig. I always look like I carried all the equipment in for Lillian's fashion shoot. I've never heard Lillian utter a swear word or raise her voice. I come into every conversation hot and drop f-bombs liberally.

What I'm trying to say is, Lillian and I have an unlikely friendship. But I'm glad we do, because thanks to Lillian, I pushed myself out of my comfort zone.

Lillian has always been good about reaching out to me. Earlier in the year she invited me to lunch and then to coffee. At both of those meetings she suggested we work together on a creative collaboration, but I didn't follow through because I suck. Lillian was trying to form a friendship and I was being incredibly reluctant. I was stuck in a rut and I had told myself I didn't have the time or energy for anything new.

But Lillian persisted. One day we met for coffee and she pitched the idea of putting together a live all-female comedy show. I had just signed the contract to write this book and I felt the pressure to spend the next year saying no to everything so I could get my writing done. (I know, this goes against all my "say yes" advice, but in my defense, I hadn't written that chapter yet and made that breakthrough.) On the other hand, I was intrigued by the idea. I'd always wanted to do some kind of live show. But I was going through so much shit, and the amount of work it would take to pull off such an event was too overwhelming. Lillian assured me she'd do all the work. To be honest, I thought nothing would come of her idea. We'd had other ideas before that had fizzled and I was positive this one would too, so I told her to give me a date and I'd show up.

That night, I was already in bed when Lillian texted me:

Want to go to open mic night with me at the comedy club?

My first instinct was to reply, "No way." No offense to Lillian, but my bra was off, my face was washed, and I was in for the night. But then I thought about Lillian and how she continued to invite me to do things with her. Yes, it would be a bit of a hassle to get dressed again and brush my hair. Yes, the comedy club was a few miles away and I might hit traffic along the way. But come on. I'd been complaining for years about how no one wanted to be my friend and this was exactly why! The fact that I look at friendship or trying new things as a nuisance is really fucked up.

I sighed and knew what I had to do. I was going to meet Lillian at the comedy club, but I was still reluctant, so I tried my last hope: the Hubs. He's a homebody too and he really doesn't like it when I'm too social because then he's left home alone and he's bored because he can't watch our Netflix shows without me. I figured he'd whine or guilt me into staying home to watch a few more episodes of *Peaky Blinders* and then I'd have the perfect excuse not to go.

"Hey, Lillian wants me to meet her at the comedy club for open mic," I said.

The Hubs looked up from his book. "Tonight?"

"Yeah, like, right now."

"Oh yeah? That could be fun. You should go."

What! "Really?" I said, wrinkling my nose. "You don't want me to stay home?"

He shrugged. "Nah, I'm going to finish this chapter and probably go to sleep. I'm pretty tired."

Ugh. The Universe was clearly telling me I should go. So I got dressed and even put on some makeup and headed to the comedy club.

When I arrived I didn't see Lillian out front.

A girl in the lobby greeted me. "Hi, are you here for open mic?"

"Yes, I'm meeting a friend," I said.

"You can go inside and see if she's in there." She motioned to the double doors in front of me. "Steve's teaching a class on how to be funny."

I went into the room and saw about two dozen people, mostly men, sitting in small groups around the room.

I still didn't see Lillian. I double-checked the information she'd given me and confirmed I was there at the right time. I was going to wait in the lobby for her, but then Steve started talking. I figured I could always use more tips on how to be funny, so I sat down to listen.

A few minutes into his presentation, I realized Steve wasn't really giving tips on how to be funny, it was more about stage presence for comics. He explained where to stand, how to hold the microphone, how to work the audience, how to use the whole stage, how to know when your time was up, that sort of thing. It wasn't what I expected, but it was interesting.

Finally, he said, "All right, that's all I've got for you guys. The show's about to start. Because you attended the class, you get three minutes onstage tonight."

I'm sorry. What? I glanced around to see if anyone else was as surprised as I was, but instead, everyone around me nodded. I had several questions and Lillian was nowhere to be seen.

Steve continued with a fairly harsh warning about how if you came in under three minutes he'd push you back up onstage and make you think up jokes on the fly ("Don't fucking waste my time") and if you went over three minutes he'd hook you off the stage ("Who do you think you are? You're not a fucking headliner!").

"All right, give your name to Sally out front and she'll put you in the lineup."

Wait. What was happening? Had I somehow signed up to be on stage? I triple-checked the text message exchange with Lillian. Nowhere in her information did she say that I would be expected to perform stand-up. She said she was considering the venue as a possibility for our show and she wanted me to see it and give her my opinion. She also thought it would be fun to watch the open mic stuff. Nowhere did she say, "Hey, Jen! Make sure you have three tight minutes ready to go, because you're going onstage tonight!"

I started to feel queasy.

"I can see some of you are looking nervous," Steve said. "That's okay. If you aren't feeling like getting up tonight, just pay the five-dollar cover charge and we're cool."

Oh my god, yes! An out! Perfect! I dug in my wallet for a five-dollar bill.

I went up to Steve with my money and said, "I'm sorry, I think I wandered into the wrong room. I'm just here to watch. I don't want to perform. Here's your money."

Everyone in the room turned and stared at me. No one else was giving Steve money. They were working on their jokes. One guy muttered, "Who the fuck wanders into open mic night?"

I get it, sir. I do. I am a fucking idiot. One hundred percent.

Steve assessed me like I was a heifer at an auction sale. "You sure you don't want to do it?"

"I am positive. I do not want to go onstage. Thank you for the opportunity, though," I said, thrusting my money at him.

Steve didn't move to take the money. "What's your name?"

"Jen."

"What do you do for a living, Jen?"

"Um, I'm a writer," I said.

"Interesting. What do you write?"

Fuck. "Humor, mostly. Actually, always. Always humor."

"You write humor?" Steve said, his eyes wide. "You any good?"

"Um, I mean, I have a pretty big social media following and, um, well, I'm a bestselling humor writer."

Steve laughed. "Cool. I'll tell you what, I'll give you *five* minutes tonight, Jen."

Fuck me. The chatter in the room immediately died and everyone was listening now. I lowered my voice. "Here's the thing, I've been onstage before. A lot. I entertain people all the time, but I'm a storyteller, not a stand-up comedian. I don't have a set. I have forty-five-minute stories I tell with highs and lows with arcs and shit!" I said.

Steve didn't say anything. I glanced around the room and I could feel the energy shift. I was making a huge faux pas.

Finally Steve said, "Stand-up is storytelling. Just give me a five-minute story and make sure I laugh."

I sighed. I'd listened to Steve's spiel and I knew five minutes was a big fucking deal and I knew all of the aspiring comics in that room would give an arm for five minutes instead of a measly three. I was being given a gift and I'd be a total dick to say "No, thank you." So I forced a smile and said, "Yeah, I can totally do that!"

I felt like I was going to throw up. I went to the bathroom and called the Hubs. "I'm doing fucking stand-up," I shrieked.

"What? For real? Right now?"

"The show starts in ten minutes or something."

"Oh wow, I thought you were just going to watch."

"So did I!"

"Is Lillian going on too?"

"She isn't here. I don't know where she is!"

"Okay, well, what jokes are you going to tell?"

"I don't know. I have five minutes. Which on one hand seems like an eternity, but on the other hand, you know me, I need five minutes just to open a story. *Fuuuuck.*"

"Just tell a funny story," the Hubs said.

"Yeah, that's what Steve said. That's not helpful."

"Just tell a story from the blog. I hate to burst your bubble, but no one in that room has ever heard of you. None of them have read your blog. It will be brand-new material to them."

Leave it to the Hubs to always keep me humble!

I made it back to my seat as the lights dimmed and there was still no sign of Lillian. Finally, she arrived a few minutes after the show started. "Sorry I'm late," she whispered. "Couldn't be helped."

"I'm going onstage," I hissed. "I have to do five minutes!"

"Oh my god, that's huge, Jen! Congratulations!"

"Why aren't you going on?" I asked.

"Oh no, that's not my thing. But you'll do great."

I finally got on stage that night at close to eleven-thirty. When the emcee called my name, all I could think was *I should be in bed by now.* But I climbed the steps and peered into the dark room.

I'd been sitting in the audience just moments before, so I knew there were only about twenty people left by then, but it still felt terrifying. Yes, I'd been onstage before in front of much bigger crowds, but a comedy club is different from a library or a corporate luncheon event. For one thing, in a comedy club the whole room is dark and you're standing in a bright spotlight so you can't see anything. I'm one of those weird people who like to see my audience. I get validation from seeing their faces. I like to see them nod along and, even better, choke with laughter. Looking into a black box made me nervous and clammy. The spotlight felt too bright and too hot on my face. I froze like a deer in headlights. The other thing that is tougher about a comedy club is that by the time I went onstage that night, the audience was made up mostly of comics who were still waiting for their turn to go up. There's a lot of whispering back and forth as people are still working on their bits. No one's paying close attention, which can be good, I guess, except I like to have an engaged audience and that audience was kind of shitty. But I took a deep breath and launched into a story about the time I won a gift certificate for a free massage when Adolpha was a toddler. It would expire in a week, so on a whim, I put the kids to bed and made a last-minute appointment. It was my first visit in years to the spa and I couldn't relax and enjoy my massage because I hadn't properly prepared myself for the visit—mentally or physically. Instead of letting go and enjoying myself, I spent the whole time hearing phantom baby cries and fretting over the fact that someone was seeing and touching my pale, jiggly, naked body complete with woolly legs and malodorous pits. I was feeling especially flatulent and I was convinced that if the masseuse kneaded me just a tad too hard, I would cut the cheese. I was so focused on my overthinking that I almost missed it when the masseuse let one rip and then tried to blame it on her shoe, like we were back in third grade or something. After that, I felt better, so I went full starfish on the table and let her work my shit out. I heard some laughter, but the one I heard the loudest was Lillian. And I focused on the sound of her laughter and pretended it was just the two of us out for coffee or lunch or whatever and I was telling her the story.

Steve had been in and out of the main room all night, so I wasn't even sure if he'd seen me onstage. I didn't care what he thought, exactly, but I would have been happy to hear his feedback. I didn't see him until I was leaving. It was way past midnight, I was exhausted, and he was deep in conversation with other people, so I wasn't going to interrupt him. I had just reached the exit when Steve called out, "Hey, Jen, if you come back on Wednesday, I'll give you ten minutes."

Lillian nudged me. "You could easily do ten minutes," she whispered. "I'll come and I'll laugh."

I went back Wednesday with a new, longer story, a bit more confidence, and Lillian by my side. I wasn't an overnight success, but I wasn't terrible either.

Soon after that, Lillian decided we'd do our show at Steve's club. She and I pulled together five funny women and started building a live act. When Lillian promised to sell out the club, I could see Steve was skeptical. (Hell, even I was skeptical, but I knew Lillian was a doer and if anyone could get it done, she could.) Lillian worked tirelessly on marketing the show and selling those seats. It was inspiring to watch her lead with such confidence and determination. If she ever doubted herself, she didn't tell me. She always looked like she had her shit together and was completely in charge. That's the amazing thing about middle-aged women like Lillian. They are fearless because they have nothing to fear. By that point in her life Lillian had accumulated years of successes and failures to learn from, and she was no longer afraid to try something new.

When the night of the live show finally rolled around, I could feel my doubt creeping in. I wasn't worried about bombing onstage. I was confident that my material was solid, and I'm at a point now where I feel like either you get my humor or you don't. So I wasn't worried about that part. I was, however, worried about filling seats. Even though I have plenty of fans who follow me online and put on pants and leave their houses to show up for my stuff, there is always a little voice inside my head that says "No one is coming," and that night was no different.

Lillian wasn't worried, because she'd been watching the ticket sales and she knew that we'd sold over two hundred seats and that it was going to be a fucking sellout. She warned Steve to stock more white wine and salad and fewer wings because ladies prefer to drink their calories. She warned the performers that we'd be going on in front of a packed house.

This story doesn't have a cute little happy ending where I tell you that I'm now a stand-up comedian and Netflix and I are in talks for my own special. Nope. This is a story about trying something scary and new and not dying. Lillian taught me a lesson about taking chances and believing in yourself even when not everyone else is on board. When Lillian first told me her idea, I didn't want to put it in ink on my calendar because I wasn't confident it would even happen. I fussed and complained that I didn't have time, I couldn't do stand-up, I didn't think anyone would come. And she still stuck with me. She also stuck with Steve even when he did not heed Lillian's advice and ran out of white wine and salad that night. Nope, Lillian persevered even with us doomsayers whispering in her ear. She put on the most successful show Steve's club had ever seen. In fact, I'm not sure anyone has topped Lillian's ticket sales to date. All because Lillian had an idea and the gumption and tenacity to try something new.

I'm so thankful she dragged my sorry ass along on her project, because it was an amazing experience to share the stage with other funny women. It was incredible to look out into the crowd (I went full diva and requested the room be a bit brighter that night) and see so many women who had chosen to come out and see us. Women who made us (and themselves) a priority that night. We entertained the shit out of them, and I know the only thing Lillian was concerned about that night was planning a follow-up event to her wildly successful debut. And I hope she brings me along on that ride too.

JEN'S GEMS

Be brave and try something that makes you uncomfortable. Say yes to terrifying things. Invite your new best friends to try something ridiculous. Stop being a fucking chicken. Be a shark. Not an itty bitty little Dwarf Lantern Shark either. Be a Great White Shark! Great White Sharks are like, "Nom, nom, motherfuckers. Get out of my way. I'm a shark. I'm not afraid of shit."

Forty Is Fucking Fabulous

And So Are Fifty and Sixty, If You Do Them Right

I know midlife can feel like it's all gloom and doom, but I promise you, it's not. Sure, everything sags, your metabolism sucks, you grow hair where you shouldn't and none where you should, you sweat like a pig, you wet your pants, and your vagina will be dry as a bone. But there is a bright side too!

Eventually you'll stop getting periods. *A-fucking-men!* Think how much money you'll save when you don't have to buy tampons anymore. No more PMS. Hallelujah! You'll be able to throw out the heating pad and the Midol. You can't accidentally get pregnant anymore and you can fearlessly wear white again.

Your nest will be empty and you'll finally have the time and energy to focus on you and what you want.

You'll have found your voice and it'll be loud and powerful.

You won't give a fuck anymore and you won't be taking anyone's shit. You'll have years of experience and decades of preparation for the next chapter in your life.

Midlife is the perfect opportunity to pivot and try something new.

I asked the women in my Midlife Bites group: "What is something you accomplished after forty?"

These are just a few of the answers I received:

Many got involved with politics.

Scarlett campaigned for several candidates.
Veronica organized her own political nonprofit.
April, Gail, Margo, and Teri all won spots on their school boards.
Julie is a parks and rec commissioner.
Irma is the chief of staff in her mayor's office.
Chantel is an assemblywoman.
Eva is a City Council member.
Rosalind is a state legislator.

A bunch made career changes.

Samantha started a new career in social work.
Melanie went after a promotion and got it.
Iyesha started her own company.
Livia was appointed a judge.
Zelda became a teacher after her kids went to college.
Rae wrote and published a book.

———

Several went back to school.

> Agnes finished high school.
> Kerry finished a degree in nursing she'd been
> putting off for years.
> Eloise earned a degree in education.
> Delphine went to night school to get her
> bachelor's degree.
> Noreen got a master's degree in computer
> science.

Health and wellness was a big one.

> Jennifer lost a hundred pounds.
> Lisa quit smoking.
> Mary became sexually adventurous.
> Dana focused on her mental health.
> Leslie started running again.
> Karen took up yoga.

Many tried new things.

> Colleen moved across the country.
> Amy took a solo trip around the world.
> Allison competed in sports.
> Debra picked up new hobbies.
> Sarah signed up for improv classes.
> Kate learned to snowboard.
> Phoebe volunteered to help refugees.
> Hilda learned a new language.
> Sonia met her birth mother.

This list just proves you are never too old to try new things. You are never too old to change careers or take up new hobbies and interests. People talk a lot about what they'd do if they had more free time, but it often ends up being a lot of talk. These women went out and did shit. Let them inspire you to get out and embrace your fabulous forties and fifties.

Ask yourself: What are you doing today to bring more joy or purpose or friends into your life? What are you doing today to move yourself closer to accomplishing the goals you've set? What could you do today to make the world a better place? Stop talking about it and start doing it.

It might feel like you're too old or you don't have enough productive years left, but that's bullshit. Instead of wasting time worrying about that stuff, I'm choosing to focus on making my future brilliant. I want to celebrate the women around me who accomplished their dreams and goals in their forties and fifties. Instead of treating a successful middle-aged woman like an inconceivable anomaly, we should normalize finding success and smashing goals after forty (and fifty, and sixty).

JEN'S GEMS

Your age isn't what's holding you back from accomplishing great things. It's you thinking you're too old. Fuck that noise. Stop talking about what you might do in the future or regretting the time you wasted in the past. Live in the present and go for it!

Energies and Auras and Spirit Guides, Oh My!

Finding a Higher Power

At this point, everyone who knows me knows I'm writing a book about my midlife crisis, because I can't stop talking about it. It consumes me. My friends and family know. My readers know. My dentist knows. The lady who helped me at the bank last week knows. My mailman probably even knows. And the first thing people do when I tell them I'm working on this book is offer me unsolicited advice.

"My mom has this roll-on hormones thing that she puts on her wrists every day or whatever. You should do that," the high schooler bagging my groceries said. Thank you, Doctor.

My dental assistant chipped plaque off my teeth while she extolled the mental health benefits of a convertible SUV. "I bought a Jeep Wrangler. Best thing I ever did. I feel twenty years younger." See? I told you the Jeep Wrangler was the female midlife crisis equivalent of a sports car!

"I embraced my cougarness," a reader said. "I haven't bought a drink in a bar since I hit forty. It's all younger men sending drinks over. My husband loves it. He thinks it's hot." I was signing her book and I almost fucked up my own name because you go, girl.

One particularly pathetic middle-aged woman said, "The kids didn't need me much anymore so I adopted a dog." That one was me. Yeah, I adopted a puppy this weekend. Stan the Mann is my perimenopausal baby. You know what? That dog gives me more hugs than my teenagers and he's always happy to see me. I know a dog will love me unconditionally and never tell me I dress like a giant toddler, which is something Adolpha actually told me the other day. Kids are fun, I should have had more!

I'm not knocking anyone's advice, though. I appreciate how hard everyone is working to try to make me feel better. No one is patting my arm and saying "It is what it is." They're all telling me what worked for them (or their mom or their neighbor's aunt). I've been trying a lot of the things they suggested. Except for the Jeep and the cougar thing. The Hubs doesn't care how unhappy I am, he refuses to let me buy me a fifty-thousand-dollar vehicle. "I let you buy a minivan because you said that would make you happy," he argues in his defense. And I could never be a cougar who gets free drinks at the bar, because I wear sensible shoes and remind the young men way too much of their mothers—or maybe it's because I *do* dress like a giant toddler. No, the dog will have to do for now.

My friend Darla had been on me to try "energy healing." We had lunch together about a week after she had her first session and she was like someone who had just found Jesus Christ her Lord and Savior and wanted to share the good news. She couldn't stop raving about her mountaintop experience and she kept encouraging me to try it. I was taken aback by her enthusiasm because I've always known Darla to be a pragmatic and logical person. I have friends who are into crystals and shit (one is even named Kristal) and they weren't half as excited as Darla. "I know you're struggling with some heavy stuff right now, Jen. I'm telling you, this shit works. A lightworker could help you navigate through all the midlife malaise you're feeling. They could point you in the right direction and help you see your way through."

Frankly, it sounded way too out there and woo-woo for me. "I don't actually believe in that horoscope stuff," I said. "It's fun to read it in *Cosmo,* but half the time it doesn't even make sense. There's always something about love on the horizon. I've been married for almost twenty years!"

Darla shook her head emphatically. "No, that stuff is garbage. You believe in a higher power, right?"

"Yes, I like God, I just don't like organized religion," I said.

"You know, I was raised going to church and then I stopped going a few years ago," Darla said. "When I had my energy session I felt more at peace and more spiritually awake than I've ever felt before. I am filled with light now."

I wanted to laugh, but I didn't because I could see how serious Darla was. She *was* kind of glowing. She reminded me of my mom when she got on a tangent about prayer. To them, it was a spiritual connection and it was serious. Even if there was no scientific basis, I couldn't deny that their beliefs in their respective higher power made them feel better. And if they weren't doing any harm, what did I care? But I still changed the subject quickly because we were getting dangerously close to Darla unloading her testimony on me and I wasn't in the mood to hear it.

Darla got deeper into her new passion over the next few months, adding Reiki and "vibrational medicine" classes to her calendar and covering every surface of her home and office with crystals.

"They provide a protective barrier between me and my difficult clients and co-workers," she explained.

"But you're still getting your flu shot this year, right?" I asked.

"Of course!" she said. "I believe in science, too, Jen!"

Each time we spoke she mentioned how much better she was feeling, physically, mentally, spiritually, but I was still positive she'd gone off the deep end and joined a cult.

So imagine my surprise when I found myself sitting across the room from an energy healer just a year after our lunch date. Darla had invited me to the smudging of her new home, a singing bowl meditation session, and a full moon ritual, and I'd said no to all of it. I knew I was supposed to be saying yes more, but I just couldn't get behind a singing bowl session, and burning sage gives me a headache. However, I admit that Darla's success with navigating her own middle-age gloom had made me curious, so I'd put out some feelers, looking for an easy introduction into energy. I didn't want to do a full-on naked howling at the moon thing with Darla's crew, but I wanted something a bit more intense than hot yoga and I knew meditation wasn't doing shit for me. My friend Kristal (of course) heard a friend of a friend was hosting an energy-slash-aura party and she was able to wangle me an invitation. It sounded like it would be a New Age Avon party. I assumed we'd have wine and cheese and get our energy and auras painted while someone tried to up-sell us on crystals and essential oils.

It was nothing like that.

I arrived at my appointed time for my private consultation where, thankfully, no one tried to sell me a healing crystal to detoxify my cellphone or some No Bad Vibes spray—although I could easily have been swayed to purchase a full moon cleansing candle. I do love a good candle. After a quick glass of wine and some cheese (yes, those were indeed on offer), I was shown into the den where a small woman sat in front of an easel in paint-covered overalls.

"My name is Elaine. I'll be painting your aura today," the woman said. She consulted the paper in her hand. "And you're Jen?"

"Yes," I said, settling into my chair on the opposite side of the room.

"Or do you prefer Jenni?"

I tried not to gasp, because Jenni is my legal name but I rarely use it except to sign contracts and checks. When I signed up for the session I purposely didn't give my last name because I didn't want Elaine to google me before our session, so I wasn't sure how she knew to call me Jenni. I wanted to ask, but I also didn't want to give anything away. I wanted to participate in this energy session because I wanted a taste of what Darla had experienced and because I figured that if nothing else, it would give me something interesting to write about. But still I remained skeptical of the whole thing. That said, within the first five seconds I was already freaked out a bit by what Elaine knew about me.

I kept my face neutral when I answered, "Jen, please."

Elaine giggled. "Okay, but your spirit guide says it's Jenni."

The fuck? I have a spirit guide? I couldn't stay quiet. I asked, "Wait. I have a spirit guide?"

"Oh yes," Elaine said, nodding.

"What are they like?" I asked, looking around as if I might be able to see them. I was kind of excited because Darla had told me all about her spirit guides. She has several, actually. Two heavily armed ancient female warriors who stand on either side of her and a tigress that stands in front of her. Her spirit guides are total badasses.

When Darla first told me about her spirit guides, I rolled my eyes. "Of course your spirit guides are badasses," I said. "Your energy healer isn't a dummy. Look at you. You're a powerful single woman with her own successful company. You sit on corporate boards and you're a leader in your community. No one is going to give you a mouse as your spirit guide and expect you to come back for another paid session."

Now that it was my turn, I realized I wanted a badass spirit guide too! I would be pissed if I got a mouse. I was hoping Elaine would give me an eagle or some kind of lady knight, or both. Or, better yet, a dragon!

"Your spirit guide is a man."

"A dude?" I screeched. "Are you kidding me?"

"He's a very, very tall man. In a white dress shirt. No tie, but it's a dress shirt. He stands in front of you at all times and keeps people away from you."

I was so disappointed. All I could think was, *My spirit guide is Jim from* The Office? *Where's my fucking dragon? I should have a dragon!*

"I'm standing behind a man?" I said, incredulously.

"He protects you," she clarified.

That didn't make me feel any better. *Stupid spirit guide nonsense.* I was over it. Now I just wanted to know how the magician did her tricks. "How do you know all this?" I asked.

"I'm an intuitive who can sense and feel things on a soul-to-soul level. I'm also a medium. I can communicate with the other side."

"You see dead people?" I joked.

Elaine didn't laugh. "Sometimes," she said.

"Do you ever stop strangers at the grocery store and say, 'Girl, dump him'?" I asked.

That got a laugh. "Sometimes."

"Oh, I would!" I said. I tried my best Whoopi Goldberg impression. "Molly . . . you in danger, girl."

Elaine smiled weakly. I don't think that was the first time someone quoted *Ghost* to her. She got us back on track. "Have you done this before?" Elaine asked.

"You tell me," I said.

She giggled again. "I'm thinking no."

I shrugged.

"Okay, let's get started. So you're going to take some deep cleansing breaths and clear your thoughts. You breathe first and then I'll breathe with you and then we'll connect."

"Right," I said. I breathed deeply and thought about the time in college a hypnotist came to campus. I wanted so badly to be hypnotized but no matter how deep I breathed or how hard I tried to clear my head I couldn't let go and go under. I couldn't relax and just be and—*the fuck was that?*

"Okay, we're connected," Elaine said.

No shit we were connected. *I could feel it.* My arms and legs were tingling and my body felt lighter. I wasn't hypnotized, but we were definitely connected in some way. I was officially freaked out. I think that's when I started crying.

"There's a tissue box on the floor beside your chair," Elaine said.

Oh good, everybody cries, I thought. *I'm not a complete weirdo.*

"Do you have any questions for me?" Elaine asked.

"No," I said, because for once in my life, I'd done what I was told and I'd emptied my brain.

"Okay, well then I'll just tell you what I'm feeling," Elaine said. "You have a giant aura."

"Yeah, I've heard that before," I said. Several people who can see auras had told me that, but they all knew me so I kind of thought they were full of shit. Either that or I think everyone is told they have a "giant aura."

"It's pushed out quite far from your body, like twelve feet or so. But you also have impossibly tight boundaries that are very close to you. But they're too tight. It's like you let people in pretty far, but when they reach a certain point you completely shut off. From everyone."

Yeah, because people are assholes, I thought. *People hurt you or suck you dry.*

"Let some of them in. Especially the ones who care about you."

"I'll think about it," I said, as I mentally reinforced my boundaries because fuck that noise.

Elaine had her back to me and was painting the canvas in front of her with thick swirls of blue and green. Suddenly she stopped and swiveled her chair to face me. "Stop it. You know you feel unhappy and alone. You won't be truly happy until you let people see your vulnerabilities, Jen. Lower your walls," she said.

She resumed painting and I grabbed more tissues, because fuck me, she kind of got me with that one.

No big deal, I thought. *Everyone has walls and boundaries and shit. This is common self-help, inspo stuff that can apply to anyone.*

Elaine spun her chair around again. "How long have you been an energy worker?" she asked.

Aha! See? She didn't know squat about me.

I laughed. "Yeah, nope. I think you missed the mark on that one."

Elaine smiled softly. "No, I didn't. I don't know what you do for a living, but you deal in energy. You are a powerful energy worker. Even right now I can feel people are plugged in to you because you give off so much energy, but it saps you because there are so many people. *Thousands* of people are plugged in to your energy every day. Does that make sense to you?"

I thought of my online community and felt my heartbeat quicken, but I kept my voice calm when I said, "Sorta."

"And you give this energy freely because you can feel their pain and you want them to feel better. You're a healer, Jen. But your supply is finite, and when you do that you deplete yourself and then you get sick and need to recharge."

I started crying again and nodded. I felt she could *see* me. She could see how tired I was. We were in month five of the coronavirus pandemic and there was no end in sight. I'd been doing everything I could to keep my followers' spirits up. I'd spent hours chatting with them, listening to them, reading to them, entertaining them, and anything else I could think of. Every night I was so wiped out I had nothing left in the tank for myself or my family.

"I can help you," she said. "You just need to ground yourself. You must get outside and reconnect with the earth."

I felt so uncomfortable. It was like I was naked in front of a stranger. When I feel trapped or scared, I make terrible jokes, so I said, "Hey! I've been bugging my husband to put in a patio, but he's too cheap. Can I say the spirits told me I need a patio?"

Elaine ignored me and said, "On particularly draining days, just take off your shoes and walk in your yard barefoot."

"Oh. Yeah, I guess that could work too. But I really want a patio." At least she didn't say I needed to get sunlight in my butthole or something. "I can do that."

"You're weird," Elaine said. I must have looked shocked because she said, "I don't mean that offensively. Stay weird. It's your superpower. Embrace your weirdness. You finally love who you are. And you need to toot your own horn."

I laughed through my tears. "I toot my own horn pretty well. Sometimes I get in trouble for my ego."

"No," Elaine said. "Toot it even more. Speak up and don't be quiet. Say what you want to say. No matter what."

"Yeah, that's not a problem," I said.

"Are you familiar with chakras?" Elaine asked.

"Only enough to make fun of them," I replied.

She ignored my defensive sarcasm and continued, "There are seven chakras. Root, sacral, solar plexus, third eye, crown, heart, and throat. Two of your chakras are very strong. The heart . . ."

I smirked. "Yeah, I don't think so. I don't have a heart," I said. I really get assholey when I'm uncomfortable.

She stopped painting again and looked me in the eye and spoke clearly. "I told you, you're a healer. Your heart chakra is very strong. You care deeply. About so many things. But your boundaries prevent others from seeing that clearly, and you're mad because no one cares as much as you do."

I didn't have a snappy retort for her, so I stayed quiet.

"Your throat chakra is even stronger. The throat chakra is all about creativity and communication. Giving voice to your opinions. And the freedom to be whoever you want to be. Yours is very strong."

Of course it is, I thought. *I'm Jen fucking Mann of* "People I Want to Punch in the Throat." *Toot, toot, motherfuckers!*

"Is any of this resonating with you?" Elaine asked.

I just shrugged. I was trying so hard to play it cool (despite all the fucking bawling), but yes, it was all ringing true.

"Do you want to talk about the project you're working on?" she asked.

"The project?" I asked, super-casually.

"It's taken you a long time but you're almost done. Just a little bit more."

There was only one project. I'd been working on this book for over a year and I'd just started on my second round of edits. The manuscript was all I'd thought about. I'd rewritten it at least twice. I dreamed about it, I worried about it, I was obsessed with it. It would be my first book that didn't fit under the "People I Want to Punch in the Throat" umbrella and I was nervous my audience wouldn't embrace it. I was afraid that all the time and energy I'd put into it would be a waste. But I didn't tell Elaine any of that. I just sat there and stared at her.

"You're on the cusp of finishing," Elaine said. "Don't be afraid to finish it."

Immediately a wave of relief washed over me, and I burst into tears again. All of the stress and anxiety I'd been carrying in my body for the past year was released. I had no idea if what she was saying would come true or not, but just hearing those words was enough to bring me comfort.

She paused for a moment, consulting her spirit guides. "Okay, this is going to sound strange, especially since we're in the time of Covid: I'm getting the word 'viral,' but not like you're sick. It's viral in a good way. Like how they say on the Internet? Have you heard that expression before?"

I nodded, barely breathing. Of course I knew that expression.

"*You're* viral. Things you've touched are viral. This is no exception. You can manifest whatever you want, but you need to stop overthinking and get the fuck out of your own way." She gasped and covered her mouth. "I am so sorry! I never curse during a session."

I laughed loudly. "Holy shit," I said. "If you're ever going to drop an f-bomb in an energy healing session, I'm the girl to do it with."

"Trust yourself. Ignore everyone else and do what you do best," she said. "You know what you need to do. Just fucking do it."

Elaine told me a lot more that day—a *lot* more—but this is what I'm willing to share so far. (Boundaries, motherfuckers.) Trust me, though, I wrote it all down before I could forget, and if any of it comes true, I'll let you know.

I'm not a convert, but I'm also not a skeptic anymore either. Sure, she told me some oddly specific things, but for the most part Elaine told me things I already knew but needed to hear someone else say to me. Sometimes I get stuck and I forget who I am and what I want and what I am capable of. I needed her to reach across the divide and telepathically slap me across the face and say "Snap out of it! You're Jen fucking Mann. Act like it!" I left our session physically and emotionally exhausted, but I also felt empowered, focused, and determined.

What this taught me is that believing in a higher power can help. I get now why my mom puts her faith in God when she's afraid and why Darla trusts her crystals to ward off negative energy. I understand why so many people feel at peace in nature or when they're surrounded by animals. As I've gotten older, I've become more open-minded about this kind of stuff and the beneficial effect it can have. I've embraced yoga and I'm (begrudgingly) working on meditation and maybe someday, if any of the things Elaine told me come to pass, I'll believe in my spirit guide. Until then, I still believe we are all connected, and I believe there are many paths you can take to get to your own personal mountaintop. Just choose the path that's right for you.

JEN'S GEMS

Magical thinking isn't always bad. Of course you should be skeptical, but you should also be open to finding the path that works for you and your beliefs. I don't give a shit what you believe in. We all need a pep talk sometimes from a religious leader, a psychic, a friend, or simply ourselves to remind us just who the fuck we are.

I'm Not Everybody's Cup of Tea, and That's All Right

Embracing All That Is You

I am constantly reminded that I am "a lot to handle" or "not for everybody." Sometimes people mean these observations as a compliment, but most of the time the person saying this to me is trying to make me change. As I get older I am more and more comfortable in my own "weird" skin and I refuse to try to fit in anymore. It is truly one of the most liberating parts of being middle-aged and I embrace it fully now.

"What's your little book about?" a man asked.

I looked up from the book I was signing and surveyed the man blocking the front of my table. He was a youngish, clean-cut white guy, no wedding band, and DAVE was embroidered on the breast of his neatly pressed polo shirt. There was a line, but Dave felt the need to push up to the front and interrupt me. I recognized him immediately.

I was in a ballroom in Michigan and I'd just given a speech to a group of city business leaders about using humor to grow an online platform. Everyone sat at round tables and ate a buffet breakfast while I spoke. Every now and again someone would get up in the middle of my time to go to the restroom or to refill their coffee, otherwise they all stayed in their seats. Except Dave. Dave stood at the back of the room frowning and shaking his head during my entire presentation. It was impossible to miss him. I saw him, but I never acknowledged him. I don't use notes when I speak, so I ignored him, because I refused to let him rattle me and make me forget my place.

I knew Dave's type. He wasn't the first Dave I'd dealt with, and I knew this conversation could go one of two ways: (1) He uses dickish behavior as a way to cover up his insecurities, but deep down he really liked what I had to say and needed to hear it, but he needs a few minutes before he can admit it, or (2) He's simply an asshole.

I finished signing the book and handed it to the woman who had paid for it. "Thank you," I said to her. Then I turned my attention to Dave. "What's it about? Well, didn't you listen to my talk? I told you what it was about," I chided, because I tend to meet hostile remarks with sarcasm. It's either sarcasm or straight to "Move on, man, you're blocking my fucking table."

He grimaced. "You spoke very fast."

I didn't argue. I had a lot to say and not a lot of time to say it.

"Well, my *little* book is actually my third book in a *New York Times* bestselling series of books." I knew I sounded braggy, but I didn't care. Dave called my book little. I held up a copy of the book and revealed the title: *Working with People I Want to Punch in the Throat*.

He frowned. "It sounds violent," he said.

"I assure you, it's not. It's humor, not how-to," I replied, motioning to the next person in line. I ignored Dave so I could speak to the man who actually wanted to buy a copy of my book.

But Dave wouldn't be ignored. "Can I at least look at one before I decide if I want it?" Dave asked.

"Of course," I replied. I indicated the stack of books beside me. "Help yourself."

He took a copy off the pile and stepped away. I saw him thumb through it, but I ignored his dramatic sighs and tsk-tsking (I assumed over my use of f-bombs like commas). My line had dwindled to only about ten or fifteen women when Dave barged up to the table yet again, ignoring the women he'd cut in front of. He held up the book. "This list," he said, shaking the book at me. "What is this?"

"It's my Punch List," I said. "I make a list for all my books. They give you an idea of the topics I'm going to cover in the essays inside."

He read aloud, "Mansplainers." He grunted and rolled his eyes.

Okay. He's a number two. He's an asshole with absolutely no sense of humor. This will be fun.

"I don't think you even know what mansplaining is," Dave snapped.

The women gaped at Dave. The sheer irony of his declaration almost killed us all.

I smiled coolly. "The fact that you're telling me that I don't know what the word means tells me that *you* don't know what it means."

I smirked at the women and they giggled.

That was all it took. I saw the shift in Dave. I watched his eyes go dark and his face go hard. If we'd been sort of ribbing each other before, now it was on like Donkey Kong. Dave wanted to go to war.

He glowered. "Oh yeah, well, what do you call a woman who thinks she knows it all?"

The women gasped softly.

"I'm a smart person who trusts women, so I'd call her right," I said, looking deep into his eyes, refusing to look away or cower.

The women chuckled.

Dave fumed and glared at me. "You're not everybody's cup of tea," he spat, his mouth curled into a mean-spirited sneer, confident in his delivery.

Here's the thing. Dave had been trying to get a rise out of me, and up until that point, I'd refused to take the bait. But I knew men like Dave. I've dealt with many Daves over the years. I write a lot of observations on everything from politics to pop culture to parenting. My opinions can be a bit polarizing at times, and although most of my readers like what I have to say, there is always someone who disagrees. No matter what I write, I tend to receive harsh criticism and backlash on just about any topic. I am known as someone who likes to "stir the pot," and sometimes when I'm at an event like that one, someone decides they'll try to stir my pot. Dave was trying to do just that.

I considered Dave's words. They were meant to hurt me. They were a jab at me. He was telling me what so many men (and even a few women) had been telling me over the years:

"Pipe down over there!"

"Shut your yap!"

"Do what you do best: Make us laugh!"

"No one cares what you think! You are nobody!"

Anytime I've crossed a line and offended or insulted or even simply irked a man with my opinion, he has been quick to lash out at me. To tell me that I'm just some fat housewife in Middle America who doesn't know shit. I've been called every name in the book, I've been threatened with violence, my family has been threatened, and yet I continue to raise my voice.

"Why?" you ask.

Because many years ago I found my voice and I found my tribe. I found that I could say the things that others couldn't. I could speak for the ones who were unable to speak up or who weren't brave enough. I could speak for the ones who felt like their ideas were meaningless. I could speak for the ones who felt alone and unseen. The ones who apologized for merely existing. I'm not everybody's cup of tea, but I'm *their* cup of tea, and that was the part Dave couldn't understand. I will never apologize for speaking my truth.

I still hadn't responded, so Dave tried again. "What do you have to say to your haters?"

I laughed. (Because so many men like Dave hate that. They hate how much space I take up, how much air I use, how loud I am, how bright I let my light glow.) "I say, who cares about them?" I snarled.

Dave was incredulous. "What? You don't care what people think of you?" he demanded. "I don't believe you! You're lying."

Fuck Dave. He didn't know who he was dealing with. I hadn't been home in over a week and I still had three more stops before I could sleep in my own bed again. I'd given that speech so many times *I* was sick of listening to my own story and hearing my own voice. I'd already been paid and the check was deposited. I'd sold all the books I had brought to sell that day, so I didn't need to be polite anymore. I didn't know anyone in that room. I would never see those people again. I was out of fucks and I was ready to end him and go find some lunch.

"You can't imagine that, can you, Dave? You can't imagine a woman who doesn't give a fuck what you or anyone else thinks. A woman who is so completely confident in who she is that nothing you say can hurt her. You are absolutely right, I am not everybody's cup of tea, and there's nothing wrong with that."

"But, but," he sputtered. "I can't believe it, but you actually sound like you're okay with that!"

"Here's the thing, Dave. There are only four people in this world whose opinions I care about, and you aren't one of them. It's just my husband, my two kids, and myself. Everyone else can go fuck themselves. You are not the first person to ask me this question and you won't be the last, but I am done trying to be everybody's cup of tea. I reach the people who need me, and those are the people I write for. I don't care if you hate what I have to say. I don't care if it bruised your ego or hurt your feelings or made you actually fucking think for a minute or whatever it was that set you off. I have no plans to change who I am, and if you don't like what I have to say, I suggest you move on and find someone else to talk to, because you are blocking my table and the people who actually want to speak to me."

I snatched my book out of Dave's hands. His mouth flapped open and closed, but no sound came out. I stared him down, unwavering. Well, inside I wavered a bit, because while I know I'm right and am not afraid to confront people, one of these days I *will* get punched in the face by some pissed-off dude, and I still had another appearance that night and I didn't want to show up with a black eye—although I would have looked badass and I'd have a great story to tell, but still.

Dave lurked around my table for the rest of the event. He challenged anyone who approached me. "What do you think of this stuff she writes?" he'd demand. Almost everyone ignored him or brushed him off. I never spoke to Dave again, and I refused to acknowledge his presence. I would not give that troll any sunlight to grow.

When I got back to the hotel that night I called my family and told them the story. My daughter was on the phone. "You have haters?" she asked, sadly.

I shrugged. "Yeah, so?"

"And you don't care?" Her nine-year-old brain couldn't comprehend. In those days she was dealing with her own mean-girl antics at school and she was working overtime to persuade those girls to be her friend. She couldn't understand the idea of writing off people instead.

"Why should I care what someone thinks of me?" I replied. "That's on them. They are the ones who spend their time worrying about what I'm up to and what I'm doing. They're the ones taking time out of their busy lives to let me know just how much they think I suck. Today Dave spent a precious hour of his life trying to make me feel bad. He's the one who wasted his time. I got work done, I made money, and I met new people. Dave is the loser here."

"But don't you want everyone to like you?" she asked. "If they don't like you, they won't buy your books. That guy didn't buy a book, did he?"

I shook my head. "I would never want him to buy my book.

He's not my people. My book is not for him. I don't write for him."

"Doesn't it hurt your feelings to know people don't like you?" my daughter said, her voice thick with emotion. I imagined the tears brimming in her eyes.

"It's taken me a long time to get to this point," I said. "That's why I need you to learn faster than I did."

"Learn what?"

"That no one can make us feel bad about ourselves unless we *let* them. No, I am not everybody's cup of tea. Dave was right about that. But do not worry about the people who don't like your tea. Find your tea drinkers. *Those* are your people."

I'm not going to lie. I wasn't always this strong. The first time I received hate mail, I cried. Hard. I was stunned that anyone could say such mean and hurtful things to me. Especially someone who didn't even know me. It's weird, I was hurt when my friends Page and Hannah didn't embrace the new me, but I was even more upset when strangers attacked me. Why did I let them bother me more? I have no idea. But I did. I lost sleep over their comments and I wanted to reply to them and defend myself.

It wasn't until I took a deep breath and a step back that I realized how foolish I was, letting myself dwell on those people. These people questioned my abilities to parent my children and they threatened to steal them. Let me say that again: Strangers on the Internet threatened to steal my kids because of a blog post about a doll. That was the turning point for me. That's when I found my strength to ask, *Who the fuck asked you?*

That's when I knew I had to work on getting tougher. I stopped giving people so much free rent in my head. That is sacred space and it's not open to the public. Then I took away their oxygen and their sunlight and let them starve from lack of attention. Don't get me wrong, I like to poke the bear sometimes. One of my favorite stress relievers is sparring with strangers on the Internet, but that is a temporary fix. Yes, I feel better for a second, but I've also let those people know they got to me. It was so much better when I learned that I didn't need to attend every fight I was invited to. Now I choose my battles. I also changed my focus. I was spending a lot of time on the one percent of the people who took time from their very busy day of picking lint from their belly button to tell me that I blow chunks. I redirected my energies into finding the people who think I'm terrific. I put all my effort into finding my tea drinkers. My goal is to find "my people," not just online but in real life too. To peel off the ones who like my brand of tea and let the others go.

This is something that's taken me more than twenty-five years to master. Twenty-five very long years. I wish my mother had told me this in kindergarten when I came home in tears because an older girl (probably a first grader, but she seemed very worldly to me in those days) made fun of my awesome striped knee socks and I refused to ever wear them again. I wish my mother had told me this in tenth grade when I moved from New Jersey to Kansas and I had to figure out how to fit my East Coast cynicism and sarcasm in with the pearl-clutching Midwestern kids. It was a hard lesson to learn, but I finally did. I don't care what others think of me. I don't try to keep up with my neighbors anymore or compare myself to my friends. I don't stress over fitting into the right wardrobe or having a magazineworthy home. I don't allow myself to suffer from mommy guilt or second-guess my parenting. I don't censor myself or make myself into a victim anymore. And I've never been happier.

I know it can sound flippant to just say "I have no more fucks to give," but it really can be that easy. That is the superpower of middle-aged women. You know who you are and what you want, so go get it. As I've gotten older, I've become a lot more confident in who I am. I recognize my worth and I'm valuable. My skills are valuable. My time is valuable. My space is valuable. My bandwidth is valuable. All of it. So I'm not letting energy vampires into my world anymore. I'm not continuing toxic relationships. I'm not suffering in silence anymore. When I feel mistreated, I speak up. When I have an opinion, I share it without fear of judgment. Because I know finding our strength always moves us forward.

You're at a point in your life now where you never need to change who you are (unless you want to)—rather, you need to find the people who like you for you. Embrace your quirks, know your strengths, celebrate your differences, find your happiness inside rather than seeking it elsewhere. Laugh at yourself, rage against injustice, be loud, be quiet, be soft, be tough, be girly, get dirty, cry, dream, imagine, work hard, have it all.

JEN'S GEMS

Midlife bites, but only if you let it!

ACKNOWLEDGMENTS

I really hate writing acknowledgments. Not because I hate thanking people (I love that part), but because I worry that I'll get all sappy, or not sappy enough. I also fret over the possibility I will leave someone out because my fortysomething brain is powered by a hamster on a wheel. So I think the best thing to do is make a list and then double- and triple-check it and then ask the hamster to take a look too.

So here's what the hamster and I came up with:

Thank you so much to my editor, Pamela Cannon. This book would not exist without you. When I sat there crying and snotting over my laptop that night, I had no idea you would read my blog post and see a book in there. Thank you for your vision, your overwhelming patience, and your guidance to help me birth this book baby. And an additional thank-you to the whole Ballantine team for your hard work and dedication to this book.

When I wrote the blog post that inspired this book, I had just parted ways with my literary agent because I felt I needed a little time on my own to figure out what the hell I was doing with my life. When the opportunity to publish this book came along, I knew I needed to find a good agent fast. Luckily, Jen Lancaster has always been a kind and generous person since the first time I stalked her at a book signing in Kansas City and declared she was my inspiration to start writing and we should be BFFs. (I still can't believe you gave me your phone number that night, Jen!) Thanks to Jen, within days I teamed up with not one, but two amazing agents. Thanks so much to Steve Troha and Erin Niumata for all your help and feedback on this book.

A year and a half ago I started the Midlife Bites Group on Facebook. As of this writing, there are 17,768 members. I am thankful for every single one of you. Each one of you has inspired this book. I don't care if you're just a lurker in there, you were vital to the process. Just the fact that you felt you needed to be there was enough to help motivate me to share my story.

And it's not just the Midlife Bites Group. I am grateful for every single person who follows me on social media. Nine years ago I was a woman screaming into the black hole of the Internet and now I'm living my dream. Thank you to everyone who ever read a blog post, shared a status update, liked a photo, or bought a book. You are my people, and I'm so happy you found me.

A huge thank-you to the Hubs. Your constant support was also vital to this book. Thank you for always encouraging me to say what I need to say. Thank you for loving me and our kids (and Stan, the dog) unconditionally. You are the best partner I could ask for.

This book took me forever and three days to write, so I need to thank my kids for making their own dinners, doing their own laundry, and constantly listening to me yell, "Keep it down, I'm trying to write a book!" I know it's embarrassing to have a mom put all her crap out there on the Internet, and I'm grateful to you both for allowing me to share our lives with a bunch of strangers. It will be easier when you're in therapy as adults. You can just hand your doctor all of my books and say, "This is why I'm here." But I hope you will always read between the lines and see that I love you both more than anything else on this planet. Now, someone take the dog out, please. He's whining and I'm trying to write my acknowledgments.

JEN MANN is best known for her wildly popular blog, "People I Want to Punch in the Throat." She is the author of the *New York Times* bestselling book *People I Want to Punch in the Throat*. She is also the editor of the *New York Times* bestselling series *I Just Want to Pee Alone*. She lives in Kansas with her husband and two children.

jenmannwrites.com
facebook.com/jen.mann.568
Twitter: @Throat_Punch
Instagram: @jenmannauthor

ABOUT THE TYPE

This book was set in Minion, a 1990 Adobe Originals typeface by Robert Slimbach. Minion is inspired by classical, old-style typefaces of the late Renaissance, a period of elegant and beautiful type designs. Created primarily for text setting, Minion combines the aesthetic and functional qualities that make text type highly readable with the versatility of digital technology.